MORE POWER TO YOU

By Charles Roth

Unity Books
Unity Village, MO 64065

Cover photo by Keith McKinney
Second printing 1987

Contents

Emancipation

No matter what has gone before, whether you have been an apparent failure or a fool, whether you have been a chronic worrier or a misfit, makes no difference. The past does not exist for you anymore, except in your mind. Starting today you can do something about it! You can erase the ugly parts of the past—mistakes, guilts, fears, failures—the same way you erase marks from a chalkboard.

The future does not exist! What you call the future is the changes that are taking place in you and around you in the ever-present now; and of course, the changes that take place around you are but an out-picturing of the changes that are taking place in you—in your mind! When you rule your mind, you rule your world.

The mind is an all-important, dynamic, critical area that contains hidden powers. Hidden, not because the Creator wanted to conceal our powers from us; quite the contrary. But hidden because most of us have not been aware of them. In fact, they are not hidden at all. The *right use* of these powers has been hidden. We have been using them blindly all along, using them ignorantly, wrongly, foolishly, and bringing grief upon ourselves.

One of these powers is emancipation. Moses was a famous emancipator. The journey of the Children of Israel to the Promised Land of peace and plenty begins with their emancipation from slavery in Egypt. So we begin our search of the hidden powers of mind with the theme of emancipation, of freedom from the bondage of false and limited beliefs that we have accepted from the outer world through our five senses, and which shackle us to lives of fear, insecurity, weakness, anxiety, and unhappiness.

When we think of slaves, we think of poor, miserable people rowing the Roman ships while the slave master beats a huge drum to set the tempo. We think of the Children of Israel working under an Egyptian overseer with a whip. We think of African people imported to pick cotton from sunrise to sunset. This is physical slavery, and mankind no longer condones it.

Yet there is another and more insidious form of slavery—mental slavery—slavery of the mind. The slave masters with the whips are Frankenstein monsters of the mind, false and limited beliefs that we ourselves have invented, built, and nourished, and to which we are now in bondage.

When we rule our minds we rule our world. But few people truly rule their minds. Who or what rules them, you ask? Statistics sometimes rule the minds of people. If, for instance, statistics say that ten out of every 100 people will get sick next month, such people will totally accept that premise as truth. It rules them. They cross their fingers and knock on wood that they won't be among the ten who get sick.

A decision to study and live Truth principles is an emancipation proclamation. A decision to live, not by the opinions and statistics of those who judge from wrong thinking and results of others' wrong thinking, but from the Truth as one perceives it deep within his own soul, is emancipation.

The first step, or the first law of mind-action, is *denial,* or the "no" law! We have to learn to stand up to our slave masters (false and limited beliefs) and say no! The word *deny* is a Latin derivative of "negara" meaning to refuse. "De" is an intensive which denotes an intense or strong refusal. To deny is *to declare untrue; to refuse to accept as true or right; to repudiate!*

Many Truth students resist the idea of

denial because they think it means stating aloud a series of negative words, thus, in a sense, giving them power. A denial isn't so much a statement made up of words, such as: *I am not sick, poor, or afraid,* it is an act of mind, an act of will. It is mentally giving an intense refusal or denying any power to a leering, threatening, whip-toting false or limited belief that looms in the shadows of the mind.

For instance, a denial is reading in the newspaper that inflation may get worse, that we are running out of gasoline, or that a depression is on its way and saying, "baloney," to the feeling that arises, making us knit our eyebrows, filling us with a sense of apprehension while this bad news sinks into our subconscious minds. If you don't think the fears radiating from a false belief are real, just notice how your first "baloney" doesn't somehow ring true. It is like shaking your fist at a tornado.

Judge Thomas Troward, a great metaphysical teacher, strengthened his power of denial by augmenting it with the law of derision. He would mockingly say, "cock-a-doodle-doo," when any outer circumstance tried to get him to believe in its power. Derision smashes a thought pattern or emotion to pieces. So when you become aware of bodily symptoms, for instance, calmly acknowledge the fact, but deny their power to hurt you. If you are sick, acknowledge the fact and do something about it as you are led; but don't go to pieces thinking the world is falling in. Don't get scared to death. Deny that the outer appearance has power to hurt you or to overcome the power of good—the power of God—that is working with you and for you. This takes spiritual courage.

If we believe that outer appearances have more power than any other power at our command, that causes fear and stress, thereby creating a greater emergency in an already weakened physical body; and sure enough, things do get worse. Don't give outer appearances power by believing that they have power, whether it be in the areas of supply, finances, human relationships, attaining a goal, or whatever. Fight back with denial, with an intense "no," with an intense refusal to bow down in supplication to its magician-like ability to make you think there is power there when there is none. There is only your belief.

Another point to consider in emancipation of your spiritual self is forgiveness. Why not start the day by forgiving everyone and everything that you have ever felt stood in your way, or hurt you, or threatened you unjustly? Do you feel guilty about anything? Forgive yourself. There's no place for self-condemnation, for dwelling on guilt over a divorce, or over how you raised your children, or that you let someone down or took advantage of them or committed an indiscretion. If you feel guilty, then it logically follows that you harbor a state of unforgiveness. You are guilty and *you* won't excuse it or let yourself forget it. That's unforgiveness; that's a lack of love; that's being hardhearted and cruel; that's being an unforgiving person! And, until you change and forgive yourself, you are going to reap the results of being cruel, unforgiving, and unloving.

How can we find forgiveness for these things that make us feel guilty? Can we undo the past? How can we get God's forgiveness? How do we forgive ourselves? Many people are hung up on this. They may have acted wrongly in the past and now they feel guilty, but they just can't put it out of their minds. There is something about guilt that makes it grow and fester the longer we keep it within us, until we feel that it is much greater than it actually is. I remember one person who confided a guilt-memory to me. I was prepared to hear something awful, something shocking. It turned out to be something that didn't seem awful at all. I would forgive her immediately for that mistake. If we would call in the first ten people who passed by and ask them if they would forgive such a mistake, I am sure they would say, "Of course we forgive you!"

If we, being far from perfect in so many respects, would forgive immediately, isn't it logical that God, who is infinite love, would forgive the moment His forgiveness was sought? There is, however, one person who wouldn't forgive this woman. This person is very nice in all other respects. She is intelligent, kind, and loving in most other cases. You guessed it, it is the woman herself. She would not forgive herself and forget.

If you are like this woman, if you intellectually and logically know that God forgives because God is love and it is not in God's nature to be unforgiving, and you still can't get rid of this feeling of guilt, of unforgiveness, of seeking ways of being punished for this mistake, of insisting on bringing it to mind so that you can punish yourself with the soothing but masochistic feelings of unworthiness and self-recrimination, then try this new approach to receiving forgiveness.

The Lord's Prayer, as rendered in the King James Version of the Bible has this to say about forgiveness: ... *And forgive us our debts, as we forgive our debtors....* (Matt. 6:12) You have probably interpreted this to mean that *if* you forgive others for what they have done to you in the past, you will receive forgiveness for what you have done to others in the past. That is valid. It is a correct interpretation. But, why is it that when you try with all your might to forgive others for what they have done to you, you still feel a sense of guilt about your own past mistakes?

Let me suggest that there is another interpretation that is just as correct and a lot more effective. It is this: ... *forgive us our debts* as *we forgive our debtors*... can also mean things that happen in the present moment *as* they happen. Forgive us our past debts or mistakes as we forgive *immediately* those who hurt us in the present moment or in some future present moment. When you forgive someone for something he did to you this afternoon, or for something he will do tomorrow, you are receiving forgiveness for one of your mistakes in the past! ... *forgive us our debts* as *we forgive our debtors....* As refers to the present moment—the now moment.

If you are living under a nagging, eroding, painful feeling of guilt about past mistakes, here is something definite, something constructive, and something effective you can do about it. Make up your mind that you are going to forgive every nasty, unhappy, cruel, thoughtless thing that happens to you *when it happens*—today, tomorrow, and for as long as you can keep it up. Things will happen to you; they are bound to. Perhaps tomorrow on the way to work you will be on a two-lane highway where there are "No Passing" lines. Up ahead is someone who is driving far under the speed limit and holding up a line of cars, including yours.

Here is an opportunity to forgive and to earn forgiveness for some of your past mistakes. So, stay calm, settle down within. Know that God's Spirit is living through the person who is driving slowly as it is through you. Whatever the reason for going so slowly, the other driver feels he has a good and right one. So let it go at that. Nothing will be lost!

You will find many opportunities to make up for your past mistakes, to resolve those guilt feelings in you. When you clean the bedroom and find your husband left his dirty clothes in a pile on the floor again instead of taking the few steps to the clothes hamper, at first a negative emotional reaction wells up. Whoops! Here is another opportunity to forgive. Smile and bless him.

You may say, of course, "I have a right to be upset with him. After all, I have to pick it up. It is thoughtless and selfish of him!" It sure is, and you are right, but that isn't the point. The point is, are you interested in finding forgiveness of *your* past mistakes and getting rid of those painful feelings of guilt, or are you more interested in being right? I did not say you should not try to correct someone who is doing something wrong. I said you should not respond inwardly with a negative feeling toward that person (anger, resentment, revenge, etc.). These wrong responses make you feel guilty later on, and they also withhold your forgiveness for your mistakes. They keep you in debt.

We think that being right gives us a good excuse or dispensation for thinking bad thoughts about another person, or for harboring a negative emotional feeling about him. After all, that slow driver *was* selfish, the husband *was* lazy and thoughtless. But did it ever occur to you that the things that you did in the past, the mistakes that you made which are making you feel guilty and unforgiven were also selfish, or nasty, or cruel, or thoughtless, and those who suffered through them feel that they have just as much right to be angry at you or unforgiving or to entertain negative feelings about you?

If you want forgiveness for yourself, you must grant it to others even when you feel they are wrong, even as you were wrong in their eyes! It seems to me that this is a healthy way of earning forgiveness. It is both unhealthy and ineffective to wring your hands and torture yourself with guilt feelings, living over and over a past mistake in your mind, pleading for forgiveness and release but actually enjoying your misery because somehow you feel this self-punishment is making up for your foolish, thoughtless, or selfish mistake.

Forgive us our debts, as we, from day to day, moment to moment forgive immediately those who do or say something that hurts us in some way or causes us to react with a negative feeling toward them. This is not just for those with an overwhelming guilt consciousness. I feel it is for all of us, myself included. We have all acted badly toward others in the past. We have thought or felt anger or hostility or resentment or jealousy toward others whether we showed it or not. We are growing. Who among us is perfect as yet? In so doing, we have been heaping up karma. Maybe nobody saw us; these anger or hostile thoughts all happen in the hidden area of the mind where no one can see. But the law sees! We cannot escape the law—the law of sowing and reaping—the law of cause and effect. And we really don't want to, because the law that brings a negative effect into our lives for every negative thought and feeling is the same law that brings good into our lives for every good, loving, forgiving thought or feeling. You will find it helpful to look for and welcome opportunities to forgive and bless others even when you feel you would be right in acting or feeling differently. Who are you helping most, the other guy, or yourself? We call this divine selfishness.

Here is another helpful hint. If I told you beforehand that I was going to say or do something nasty or irritating to get you upset, you would be prepared, and when I did it, you would think, "Ha, there he is doing it, just as he said, trying to get me upset. But I am ready. I won't get upset." Well, things are going to happen to you today, tomorrow, and next week which will tempt you to get upset, angry, and resentful. You know this and you can be prepared. When the boss gives you a curt, "Good morning," and never mentions the big contract you pulled off for the company yesterday, instead of reacting with injured pride and thinking dark and ugly things about the boss, you will say, "Well, there's the first one today. Thought you would upset me, eh, get me wallowing in negative emotions, originating a negative cause which will produce, by law, a negative effect in my life. Well, I'll fool you. I forgive and bless."

I guarantee that if you go through just one day forgiving immediately, and not getting upset or responding emotionally toward any person or circumstance that hurts you in any way, you will come out on top. So clear out the garbage of unforgiveness of yourself and others that is expressing as unpleasant conditions in your life with this affirmation: *From the bottom of my heart and soul I forgive myself and every person or condition that I have pronounced guilty of wrongdoing.* This doesn't mean you condone it; it merely means that you understand it. You hold nothing against that person or condition, or yourself. Greater is the power within you to overcome whatever condition that seems to cause you hardship or any person who knowingly or unknowingly hurts you, or any mistake that you make. Greater is that power within you than the person, condition, or mistake!

Proclaim your emancipation now. Deny that any condition or circumstance has power to make you upset, angry, or resentful at *any situation or person*—including yourself! *I overlook and forgive immediately. I act with calmness, firmness, and kindness. I am grateful!*

Will

The chief executive, the prime minister of the kingdom of mind, is the faculty of will. It says go; it gives the order for action. If we are going to rule our minds, we are going to have to educate our will.

All power flows from God, the universal sense of Being, through our individual sense of I Am. But, and here is where the rub comes in, that power is expressed through the will, and this faculty can be incompetent, ill-informed, and inefficient.

The undifferentiated God-power flows to our sense of "I," our changeless, ageless individuality. From there our will directs it into specific action. For instance, we can think, "I (the power source) will (the power director) respond to this situation with anger." The one Power then becomes a destructive force increasing our blood pressure and heartbeat, pouring adrenalin into the bloodstream, and placing our bodies into states of stress.

On the other hand, when we think "I (the power source) will (the power director) remain calm and seek guidance from within," the one power becomes a beneficent force, enabling us to think clearly and be receptive to the light of Truth within. So you can see why it is necessary to train the faculty of will to respond rightly.

You may object that you didn't "will" to get angry; it was a compulsive, seemingly automatic response. The answer to that is that the prime minister (the will) has a computer. After "willing" in a certain direction in response to a given set of circumstances, that response is programmed into the computer (the subconscious mind). This saves a lot of decision making. For, every time that circumstance arises, the computer automatically will set the previously programmed decision into action. We have to train the will to quickly push the "cancel" button when this happens, and make a new and more spiritually oriented decision.

It isn't easy to cancel or abort a response from the highly efficient subconscious computer. The best way I have found is to determine (will) that there is a three-second delay before I react to any outer stimulus. In that interval I have time to "will" to be receptive to guidance from the light of understanding within. So how can we educate our prime minister so that it will express or direct that power beneficently instead of destructively? Let's get down to the nuts and bolts of living by using the example of dieting.

Dieting seems to be a very common challenge. Diet books are bestsellers. Nationwide organizations for people seeking weight control methods are popular. John and Mary Doe are overweight, and they aren't happy about it. They both have read books on dieting and have memorized just how many calories different foods have. John and Mary go into a restaurant and order a huge lasagna, and to top that off, they order a rich dessert. In their kingdom of mind, the prime minister said, "I will to order lasagna and dessert." This was a poor decision on the part of the prime minister. It could only lead to finding more "storage space" in the already bulging warehouses of their bodies. Why did they will to do it? It wasn't so much that the will was weak (as we usually say), or even that the decision was an automatic "subconscious computer" response. There was an adequate interval to make a right response. In this case, as in many instances, the prime minister (the will) was poorly informed by his department heads.

There are five components in an act of will—we call them department heads—whose information or input is necessary to an intelligent, beneficial act of will. We have the *desire* department, the *research* department, the *decision* department, the *affirmation* department, and the *planning* department. Every act of will, every action you take, has gone through these five departments. The trouble with an action you take that is not wise or beneficial is that it did not get proper attention in one or more of these departments. For instance, in the John and Mary Doe example of dieting, how deep, how strong is the *desire* to diet? Is it a wish, a hope, a yearning. Or is it a dynamic and relentless power of *desire?*

John and Mary have to be honest with themselves. Maybe they really feel they are not that overweight. They need to work with their *desire* departments by picturing how they will look and how their lives will be if they don't diet. Then they can picture how they will look if they do diet. You see, *desire* is a motivating power. Motive is another name for desire. Motive gives direction to the will. If our motive (desire) is to make money, our lives move in that direction in every way. If our motive is to get well, to write a book, or whatever, our lives move in that direction. So, if introspection reveals that our *desires* aren't all-consuming and strong, and our will orders lasagna, we must not be surprised or blame a weak will. The *desire* department voted in favor of lasagna against winning the battle of the bulge. The will didn't have the powerful backing of the *desire* department.

Next, we have the *research* department. This is the "is it possible at this point" department. Perhaps with dieting, there isn't too much to consider here unless one weighs 500 pounds and has a goal to weigh 100 pounds—that would be an imposing challenge. But in many acts of will, *research*, or "is it possible at this point," is very important. I have seen many Truth students and even Truth ministers who charged forth crying, "Everything is possible with God!" and later found that they had bitten off more than they could chew. The time was not right, or they did not have enough foundation. They needed *research*. "What is involved in this goal or desire that I am considering?" we must ask.

In the *decision* department we weigh the cost. Every choice or decision necessarily involves renunciation, or a cost. For instance: If we eat cake, we may be renouncing the experience of living in slim bodies. If we don't eat cake, we renounce the satisfying taste of a rich, delicious cake.

Although prayer and meditation should be incorporated into all five steps or departments, I feel it is most important here. *Decision* is a crucial step, and we should take time to earnestly seek guidance. If and when we get that, we have an unearthly Power, a miracle-working Power working for and with us. We will know deep down that this is the right thing to do, and we will feel that God is saying, "Yes, you have my help."

The die is cast in the *affirmation* department as we affirm: *With God's help I am going to achieve this goal.* Visualization also increases the power of an affirmation. See yourself experiencing your goal.

No matter what our goals or desires, we have to have a plan, or we might wander off course. So finally we have the *planning* department. If our goal is to wake up full of energy in the morning instead of dragging around, we must plan to program our subconscious minds before going to sleep. If the goal is to take off so many pounds, we can plan to reward ourselves for every five pounds we take off. We should also plan to praise our bodies for working with us. And it is very important that we plan our shopping, and our menus.

Planning is also important in considering possible or foreseeable contingencies. Thus, if things go wrong, our wills do not collapse; we will have alternate plans ready. Think about what you want more than anything in the world! Is it fame, a big house on the most exclusive avenue in your city, to have your name as well-known as a movie star? Do you know what you want?

That brings up one of the reasons that we may not feel fulfilled and good inside—we don't know what we really want. Think about it for a moment while I tell you a story. Just what do you really want out of life?

Frank Peterson was a mail clerk. He had nothing against his job. It paid fairly well even if he was always broke because of his mismanagement, and the high cost of living, and many other excuses. After all, he made more money than a lot of people he knew. But deeper than the money, he felt unfulfilled and incomplete. Then one day he ran across one sentence in a book he had borrowed from the library. It said: *No successful house was ever built, no successful sale was ever made, no successful life was ever lived without a plan!*

"Plan," he said. "What have I to plan?" But the idea wouldn't let go of him. So he decided to plan what he would do on his next weekend off. He wrote it down. He thought about the things he absolutely had to do, and it occurred to him that it would be a good idea to get them out of the way first so that he could let his imagination run loose on how to design a really good weekend. It took him about an hour to make his plan, and he began to look forward to Friday evening so he could put it into effect.

The plan worked like a miracle. Although he thought it would be difficult to follow it, he overlooked a basic law of mind-action. When you drop a plan into the subconscious mind by thinking it out and better yet, by writing it out, the subconscious mind goes to work to help you carry it out. The result was one of the most interesting and productive weekends of his life. He then began to plan his work days and his free time. He never felt chained to the plans. If something unexpected came up, he adjusted the plans. He had read something about non-resistance and decided that he would not resist interruptions or unexpected developments but would make friends with them. A friend can't hurt you, he reasoned.

Frank became a changed person. He looked more poised and confident, and he felt the same. He had the look and feel of a man who knew what he was doing and who knew that he was capable.

Because life is consciousness, and when we

change our consciousness our lives change, it wasn't long before an opportunity for another job came along. It was a challenging job, but if he did well there was no ceiling to his remuneration.

Frank took a six-month leave of absence and gave it a try, continuing to apply his "life-renewing" theory of planning. Today, Frank Peterson's salary is quite high. His family has the things that make for a full life; and a spirit of love and joy pervade the Peterson household such as he never dreamed possible.

Now the thing that seems important to think about in this true story is: Frank didn't start with a definite final goal in mind. He started with a success principle—the principle of planning. You see, many times we don't really know what it is that we want as a final goal. Earlier I asked you to think about what you really want out of life. No doubt you couldn't pinpoint exactly what you wanted.

Let the final goal wait. Let it develop. Start where you are, using the principle of planned living. Would you like to clean out of the house all those unproductive things you saved for years? Make a plan. Would you like to get the yard and grounds in better shape? Make a plan. Would you like to get your office work reorganized on a more efficient system? Make a plan!

In the Bible we read: *Thou shalt also decree a thing, and it shall be established unto thee. . . .* (Job 22:28 A.V.) What do you suppose this means? The average Bible reader probably would skip over this passage, thinking it doesn't apply to him. Perhaps it is the word *decree* that throws him off the track. "Only kings or people in power decree things," he might unconsciously reason. "And that's not me!"

But that's just the point. You are a child of God, the child of a King. You are created in the image and after the likeness of God. Your human self may be someone whom you consider unimportant, but the spiritual you is of royal blood. The principle of planned living is merely a practical way of applying this Bible promise. Your mental design or plan is your decree. Writing it down strengthens that decree and impresses it in the working area of mind—the subconscious phase of mind—or what the Bible calls the heart.

Then, of course, you must take action. You will find action comes much easier when you know what you want to do and have the blueprint before you. Let me give you some positive examples of the use of this success principle for planning. Perhaps they will kindle ideas in you for adapting the law to your own life and circumstance.

The first example that comes to mind is an insurance salesman who sold as much insurance in two months as he had sold in the ten previous months by setting up Saturday morning as his planning time. He would plan the following week, not just who he would see, but he would think about his contacts and their backgrounds and needs, and he would plan what he wanted to say to them and how he would say it. He found, just as I have found and you will find, that it works like magic. He worried less; he sold more; he did a more effective job of presenting himself; he felt more confident, poised, and relaxed.

Here's another way to apply the law in your life. Take the first five or ten minutes after waking up just to lie in bed, picturing in your mind the day ahead of you and "seeing" yourself accomplishing the things you have to do, easily and successfully. Does this sound too simple and good to be true? Try it. You'll find that it works.

Another person used this plan in buying a new suit. This is sometimes a challenging experience. Would he get a good salesman who knows what is best for him? Would he find the suit he wants? Before going to the clothing store, he stopped at a drugstore for a cup of coffee. He sat there and pictured himself going into the store, and he pictured the best salesman taking care of him and finding the perfect suit. Did it happen that way? Believe me, it did.

You may be thinking, "How can little, relatively unimportant things, such as lying in bed for a few extra minutes planning your day, or taking time to imagine yourself going in to buy a new dress or suit or car have anything to do with the larger goals, the more important goals of happy and fulfilling living?"

As I have experienced life, they have a lot to do with it. I can only talk for me, out of my life experience, and the way my mind works. Perhaps all of us have a lot of mental attitudes, both hang-ups and good points, in common. I, personally, cannot deal with or think in terms of long-range goals. There is no way in the world that I could have conceived the goal of being an author, a minister, or a world traveler when Elizabeth, my wife, and I were busy taking care of three children, wheeling in coal from the street where the truck dumped it, and shoveling it down the shute in the cellar window in Buffalo, New York, some thirty years ago.

However, I can handle short-term goals, such as planning a weekend, buying a car, reading up on a certain subject that interests me, or finding time to study a correspondence course. So the way I figure it is: God in me, Spirit in me, the Christ in me knows my long-range goals. God in me also knows me inside out. He knows that I cannot think in terms of long-range goals. So God in me keeps putting in front of me the consecutive short-range goals that are a necessary part of the path to the long-range goals. Therefore, all I have to do is take the short-range goals as they come into my life and, doing my best to keep that inner contact with Spirit through meditative prayer and spiritually-oriented thinking, work at them with the planning principle. Lo and behold, in five years or ten years, or whatever, there I am at a goal that I would never have dreamed possible.

As I said earlier, when you drop a plan into the subconscious mind by thinking it out, or better yet, by writing it out, under the law of mind-action the subconscious mind goes to work to help you carry out the plan easily, effortlessly, and successfully. Start with some relatively small or seemingly unimportant job or goal facing you at present. Apply the success principle of planning and turn it over to the prime minister, the will, after you have *desired, researched* for its feasibility, *decided* with God's "Yes!" *affirmed* with assurance, and *planned* with imagination and wisdom. These five steps are valid only to the degree that you apply them in your life—only to the degree that you do them, not just read about and agree with them, but actually put them into action in your daily living.

Decree

You have, at the tip of your tongue, the power to mold circumstances. The Bible assures you of this power in Job 22:28: *Thou shalt also decree a thing, and it shall be established unto thee.*

Decree simply means decide. Should we go out to eat, or eat at home? The decision is made in your mind, and action follows. The important factor is the decision. The action follows the direction of the decision.

You can decide (decree) that this is a hostile universe, or indifferent at best, and you will find circumstances continually working against you. Or, you can decide (decree) that this is a friendly universe, and your path will be pleasant and harmonious. It will, according to your decree, be established.

Affirmations are powerful mental tools. They help us to make right decisions. We may want to decide to trust God instead of giving in to the seemingly overwhelming power of an outer condition, but the churning emotions of fear and helplessness hold us prisoner. This is the time to remember our power of decree. An affirmation is a decree. It is the announcement of a decision. So, we might affirm: *There is only one Presence and one Power, God the good, Omnipotent. God wisdom in me is my dependable source of inspiration, direction, and success!* Hold to that decision, and action toward a successful outworking of the condition will follow.

When I first started a radio ministry I had plenty of opportunities to use my power of decree. Radio stations were a new experience to me, and a bit terrifying. My heart would pound, and my hands would perspire, and the butterflies in my stomach would have a field day as I approached the studio. I would affirm over and over: *I am centered and poised in the Christ Mind; nothing disturbs the calm peace of my soul!* And always, I would feel quiet, composed, and ready to do what was mine to do without tension or anxiety.

In a health challenge, decree God's healing power and presence. One Sunday morning I arose before anyone else in order to finish work on my Sunday lesson. I felt strange physically—dizziness and a fast heartbeat. All sorts of negative imaginings popped into my mind. I remember lying down on the floor and repeating over and over: *There is only one Presence and one Power, God the good, Omnipotent. That power is working through and for me now.* After what seemed like hours, but was probably only ten minutes of continuous affirming, I felt normal again.

Words are dynamite. Thoughts and words have molding power. You can talk yourself into trouble by the careless use of words. Solomon knew the power of words when he wrote: *The wicked is snared by the transgression of his lips. . . .* (Prov. 12:13 A.V.) This could be interpreted to refer to lying. But I am sure wise old Solomon meant more than the obvious results of lying. He meant you would be "snared" or caught up in big trouble by negative, limited, lack-oriented, or illness-oriented words that pass your lips.

Further in Proverbs, Solomon wrote: *A man's belly shall be satisfied with the fruit of his mouth. . . .* (Prov. 18:20 A.V.) What else is the fruit of your mouth but words! Just as the previous passage told of the destructive power of negative words, this passage reveals that the principle works both ways: Good is attracted into your life by positive, Truth-oriented words.

We have heard Job, who became wise the hard way, tell us of the power of decree. We have considered Solomon's proverbs on the formative power of words. Now let us turn to the prophets. Jeremiah wrote: *"But 'the burden of the Lord' you shall mention no more, for the burden is every man's own word....*" (Jer. 23:36) Jeremiah is really laying it on the line. He is saying, "Don't blame God for your troubles. It is your own words, the fruit of your own lips, that bring burdens on you."

In this day and age we sometimes blame God, but we also blame inflation, the President, big business, big unions, and so on for our troubles. We don't like to hear the prophetic voice of Jeremiah in us saying, "Your words are bringing on your troubles. Stop complaining and blaming, and start looking for what's right. Give thanks for what you have. Start decreeing good for yourself instead of decreeing more trouble!"

Then we turn to the New Testament, and the words of Jesus ring in our ears: *For by thy words thou shalt be justified, and by thy words thou shalt be condemned.* (Matt. 12:37 A.V.) I don't think the awesome power of your word can be described more succinctly or dramatically than that.

Words have a unique power to vibrate against the sensitive ethers, or substance, or primary energy in which we live, move, and have our being. They bring into manifestation conditions that are of their same character. For example: Talk for about ten minutes with someone to whom you have just been introduced. You will have a pretty good idea about that person's world, whether it is happy or trouble-filled; whether the person is successful or defeat prone; whether the person is healthy and energetic or chronically sick. Where do you get this information? You get it through the words he speaks and the way he speaks them.

Conditions are effects, and every effect has a corresponding cause. Thought, which is expressed through words, is cause. If you want to change something in your life, it is useless and pointless to work in the realm of effects. It is a waste of time and emotional energy to try to force things or to manipulate people to do what will make you happy or successful. To change the condition, change the cause. Change your thinking and let your words reflect that new way of thinking.

Picture a tall building under construction in the distance. There are hundreds of, what seem from our vantage point, little workers scurrying about, busy at one thing or another. We can't see exactly what they are doing, but each day and each week the building takes on a more and more completed form. So it is with the words you speak. They are like little workers. When you speak words of health, energy, vigor, strength, faith, and order you are employing little skilled workers who go to work doing one thing or another toward carrying out the blueprint or the character of the thought encapsuled in the word. I said *doing one thing or the other* to point out that we cannot see precisely what each worker is doing, but we know it is something good and important because the building is taking perfect form. Even so, we are not aware precisely of all the minute but necessary changes that are taking place as our words build or form new conditions in our lives.

But now we come to an equally important point: There are worker words and there are vandal words! How sad it is to read of vandalism in the papers, or even worse to see the work of vandals—broken windows in a house that was once a warm home; perhaps the charred remains of a house; or scrawled obscenities on a beautiful building. We don't even like to think about such things. But friends, when we decree from our minds thoughts encapsuled in words such as *tired, weak, failure, old, I can't,* or *hopeless,* well, you know the breed—these are vandal words. They will make a mess of our lives. They will impoverish our environmental conditions as well as vandalize our bodies.

Matthew reports these words of Jesus: *"I tell you, on the day of judgment men will render account for every careless word they utter...."* (Matt. 12:36) The "careless words" that Jesus speaks of are "vandal" words. Vandals are careless people. They are so inwardly empty and so addicted to outer excitement that they feel they will "go nuts" if they don't find some new outer excitement to give them a "high." So they drive over lawns or break windows or get their kicks from some sort of destructive activity.

Even so, many people get a "kick" out of speaking complaining words about how poor they are, or how sickly and weak, or how life has treated them so unfairly, while a seemingly unworthy neighbor prospers and gets all the breaks. Those are vandal words, careless words, destructive words. And such persons always get bad deals on judgment day—which is every day. Judgment day is any day on which previously held thoughts and beliefs are objectified as conditions and experiences. Today is judgment day in that you and I are reaping or experiencing the results of what we said, thought, and believed in the past!

But all too many of the people who receive bad news on their judgment days refuse to learn from it. Instead they use the unhappy judgment day conditions as an excuse for speaking more idle words of self-pity, anger, hatred, envy, and resentment.

All of us from time to time have unhappy or challenging conditions in our lives, and we are liable to feel guilty or embarrassed by having to admit that we brought much of it on ourselves by our thoughts and words. Well, we are growing, we are learning. Maybe we do have rough, challenging, hard conditions in our lives, but we don't have to talk about them and go over and over them, telling every Tom, Dick, and Harry about our troubles. If we do, we will never get out of what Solomon calls the snare because we are fastening the negative conditions to us by our words.

Here is a good tip that I learned years ago from a Unity student from Puerto Rico. He said, "I used to lovingly ask people when I met them on the street, 'How are you today?' But I'd inevitably get a long recital of ills, of all the negative situations in their lives. So now I ask, 'How is your faith today?' It usually surprises the person, but the answer is affirmative. It calls for an affirmative reply."

All words are important, but there is a special class of words that you could call "power words." Power words are words that have an extra charge in them, an extra spiritual charge, an atom-influencing charge. A tremendous power term is "divine order." When things look confused and as if they are going all wrong, you need only say *divine order,* and you will immediately begin to reverse the flow of things. You see, this is a very simple and practical application of the Bible principle: *Thou shalt also decree a thing, and it shall be established unto thee.*

If we would try to analyse the divine order power word, we would find that the first thing it does is reverse or at least stop the negative thinking about the disorderly condition confronting us. I have had many examples of this in my own experience. There have been many at airports—planes are late, or the weather is bad, and I have felt myself getting tense and uptight, picturing all the trouble ahead. "Why doesn't the airline do this or that?" Then I remember to say, "Everything is in divine order!" As I repeat those power words, I can actually feel more peaceful. I relax, usually smile a bit, and the first thing I know, the troublesome circumstance is in the past. It is behind me, and it all worked out for the good!

Now there is more to power words than just the spiritual power in the word itself. There is a sense in which the power of our own personal consciousness—our spiritual consciousness—is poured into the word. You see, every time we attend a Truth lecture, every time we read the Bible, every time we read our DAILY WORD, we are building an ever-increasing, ever-stronger spiritual awareness; an increasingly larger and stronger thought-complex of spiritual understanding and faith. So when we use spiritual power phrases, such as: "Peace be still"; "Divine order"; "Christ in me is my strength"; "The Lord is my shepherd"; or "There is only one Presence and one Power," the original spiritual charge in the power is amplified by all those spiritual thoughts that have passed through our conscious minds and remain in our subconscious minds.

For instance: A Unity student was in a serious auto accident. He told me that when it happened his first thought was "God is here." That was a power phrase for him. All of that spiritual understanding in the storage bins of the subconscious level of his mind came pouring through those words and into the situation. It is a power that influences for the good the physical or material conditions that we think are so unchangeable, or are only influenced by other outer forces or luck. How, I don't know exactly. (Even physical scientists don't know how certain things happen, but they know they can scientifically count on them happening.) This Unity student told me that he was taken care of at the time in a divinely orderly and divinely timely way, and he got well so fast that his recovery seemed miraculous.

As we grow in spiritual understanding through meditating habitually, we can construct our own power words for different situations. For instance: For times when we are tired or lethargic and don't feel like doing what needs to be done, we can develop subconscious spiritual power around the word *now*. Meditate on spiritual ideas, such as: *Universal life energy is flowing through me now. I feel it;* and *I am alive, alert, awake, and enthusiastic, now!* We can decree to our subconscious minds that every time we say the word *now* the power of all these spiritual ideas will come into action. And by the very act of decreeing, whatever is needed is accomplished—*now!*

To sum up: Words are not just the sweet, bland, innocuous things that we may think they are. They are so common. Books are full of them. We are constantly hearing and using them. They are "just words." But words are deceivingly powerful! It is commonly accepted that thought is a formative power. That formative power is multiplied by compressing the thought or belief into a word or words. Words are amplifiers, especially when charged with feeling. Just as an amplifier takes almost inaudible sound signals from a record and amplifies them until they can fill the room and vibrate the walls, so does a feeling-full, spoken word—as Jesus said, spoken in faith and without doubt in the heart—amplify the power of thought and cause the very ethers and atoms to tremble and conform to the character of the encapsuled thought.

Worker words or vandal words—the power of decree is ours!

Wisdom

There is a vast difference between knowledge and wisdom. Knowledge is an intellectual possession. It is gained by gathering information, by accumulating facts, and by other people's opinions. We gain knowledge about a variety of subjects by reading books, attending schools, performing experiments, collecting statistics, and so forth.

Knowledge is quite fashionable these days. I know people who have gone to school until they were thirty years old. They collect letters (B.A., M.A., PhD.). When you add up all the letters, they spell knowledge with a capital "K." But wisdom is something else. We cannot get it out of a book. Wisdom is of such a nature that it cannot be imparted from without. It can only originate from within.

It is wisdom, not intellectual knowledge, that is the key to happy, successful, and abundant living. In the third chapter of Proverbs the writer makes such fabulous promises of what wisdom will do for you that he could be the envy of Madison Avenue publicity writers. He says: *Happy is the man who finds wisdom . . . for the gain from it is better than gain from silver and its profit better than gold. She is more precious than jewels, and nothing you desire can compare with her. Long life is in her right hand; in her left hand are riches and honor. Her ways are ways of pleasantness, and all her paths are peace. She is a tree of life to those who lay hold of her; those who hold her fast are called happy.* (Prov. 3:13-18)

The writer of this passage is saying that if we develop our innate faculty of wisdom, we will live long; experience riches and honor; our lives will be pleasant (satisfying in every respect); we will have peace of mind. *She is a tree of life* means that, not only will we live long, but we will be continually renewed with energy, strength, and health; and we will find happiness, *for those who hold her fast are called happy.*

Why do you suppose the Bible refers to wisdom as "she"? *She is more precious than jewels . . . . Long life is in her right hand and in her left hand are riches and honor.* In the metaphysical interpretation of the Bible, a feminine character always represents the soul or feeling nature in one of its aspects. A masculine character in the Bible always metaphysically represents some phase of the will or intellect. Metaphysically the feeling nature is feminine—the intellect, masculine; heart and head, feminine and masculine. So the Bible, referring to wisdom as she or feminine, is subtly pointing out that wisdom is not gained through intellect but through the soul or feeling nature. It is not gained from without but from within!

Our knowledge is growing at a fantastic pace, but wisdom, the inner information that brings true satisfaction, love, freedom from the fear of lack, and all the other good things that we all secretly long for, is sadly lacking in the world today. Perhaps some of the reasons for this is that the world demands so much of our time that we have less and less for privacy, for solitude, for those delicious few moments of just being alone to think our own thoughts and to let gems of wisdom unhurriedly arise in our minds.

It is time that we who have glimpsed this potential of the hidden power of the mind came to our senses and put first things first. Sure it is important that shopping be done, the house cleaned, the work at the office be taken care of, and the outer details of living be handled. But it is more important that we take time to relax in the midst of the rushing moments of life and seek wisdom from within, from God. But first we have to convince ourselves that it is just as possible, just as legitimate, just as normal to receive wisdom from within our own beings as it is to receive it from outside sources.

This is more difficult for most of us than it sounds. We have limited and false self-images built up about ourselves in our subconscious minds. If we are honest about it, we often don't think very much of our own opinions and ideas. If we read something in books or hear someone with a lot of letters after his or her name say something, we accept it almost without question; but of thoughts or feelings that arise within us? "Well," we apologize, "of course, it is only what *I* think."

You are a child of God! You are created in the image and likeness of God! Do you think that when you read in the first chapter of Genesis that God created man in His (God's) own likeness it means everybody except you? That would make you exclusive, but who wants to be that exclusive? You are remarkable. You are wonderful. You have potential that staggers the imagination.

In order to gain that which is better than silver and gold—more precious than jewels— we have to have what we might call "informed humility." This is an inner realization of who and what we are as children of God, spiritual beings, the "spittin' image" (to pharaphrase the first chapter of Genesis in my grandmother's vernacular) of God. That's the informed part. The humility part is recognizing that this remarkable, wonderful being with the tremendous potential that you are needs to work with God.

With an informed humility state of mind as the starting point, let's think about ways or techniques of making ourselves receptive to the wisdom that makes for truly successful living; the wisdom that not only solves problems, big or small, but delights in problems as opportunities to grow and to gain even more wisdom.

The first technique has to do with problem-solving, and it is very simple. It is: Arrange to have times of solitude in your life. Solitude and privacy are the most suitable conditions for wisdom to arise into the conscious mind from the subconscious and superconscious levels. As an example, if you are studying this lesson while you are completely alone, you are likely getting much more out of it.

Remember this principle: When you really want to think, when you want to work something out in your mind and you want the benefits of your superconscious mind working with you to give you ideas or insight that you don't presently have, "Go apart a while,"

as Jesus taught and did. Take a drive or just
find some excuse to go to your room and shut
the door so you won't be disturbed. Don't try
too hard to think or even to pray. Just relax
into the silence around you. Yes, there may
be children shouting in the yard, or horns
blowing, but there will seem to be a wall of
separation, invisible, but real.

Have a paper and pencil with you. This is
very important. Writing is a way to clarify
your thinking, to impress your subconscious
mind. You must pinpoint your problem. Say
to yourself, "Now, let's just see if I can put
the real heart of my problem into not more
than three sentences." This helps you to take
an objective view, to subtract yourself emotionally from your problem, to view it as just
a problem instead of *your* problem.

Your purpose is not to solve the problem
but to state the problem. You will find yourself getting all enthused about the challenge
of trying to put this very real problem into a
clear sentence or two. In the process of doing
this, many things will happen. From within
you will arise a new understanding of the
problem. Perhaps you will see that what you
thought was the heart of the problem isn't at
all. Perhaps it was your reactions, rather
than another's actions, that is the key to a

workable solution.

Also, jot down any thoughts or ideas that come to you while you are creatively contemplating the problem. For instance, the title of a Sunday lesson, "Love, Don't Shove!" occurred to a Truth student. As he penciled the words, a surge of insight brought him a new viewpoint that proved important.

Another person found a favorite albeit rather unorthodox affirmation of a friend of mine occurring to her. It was: *Who cares?* When she reexamined her problem she found that much of her tension-producing concern was over what other people were saying or thinking. It is pleasantly surprising how often the two words: *Who cares?* can put things in proper perspective.

Wisdom is not some special spiritual language understood only by mystics. Universal Mind speaks to you through your mind and thoughts using the contents of your own life experiences as its carriers of wisdom.

When you read a book and a particular sentence or phrase strikes a responsive chord in you, write it down. This will make it yours and it adds to your subconscious storehouse of potential wisdom carriers. Reading a book might be compared to shopping in a furniture store. Every item is available to everyone and anyone—except those items that have a "sold" tag. The word-encased ideas in a book are available to every reader, but when you find an idea that "rings a bell" for you, and you write it down, it becomes your personal property in a very special way. I have even found potential words of wisdom while watching television, and have hurriedly gone for pencil and paper. If we can find sermons in stones, why not potential wisdom carriers in a television show?

Problem solving isn't the only activity in which to seek wisdom. One of wisdom's many children is creativity. I know a nurse who arises early enough to spend thirty minutes of the quiet morning hours at the kitchen table just letting her mind dwell on her work, on people, and on circumstances in her life. She discovers new ways to be more efficient and to serve better at work, and to enrich her own life in various ways.

Whether it be creative problem-solving or just musing over a cup of coffee in the early hours of the morning, you will emerge from your time of solitude and privacy renewed in mind.

Another suggestion for increasing your store of wisdom and thereby enriching your life is to keep your own Wisdom Book. At the end of each day, or at a regular time set aside for it, write down in a notebook the date at the top of a new page, and under the date write: "Today I learned that ..." Quietly think of the new experiences you had that day, the phone calls, the luncheon conversations. Review your day and uncover what lesson, what Truth you learned through the experiences.

Here are some sample notes from the Wisdom Book of a business executive I know: *Today I learned that a phone call will get a problem off my mind and on its way to a solution. Do it now!* Now you might say, "I know that!" Sure, so did the man who wrote it in his Wisdom Book. But during that day he had made a phone call about a problem that had been aggravating him for weeks. When it came time for his Wisdom Book session he remembered the relief he felt after the phone call and he reproved himself for not doing it earlier. So he wrote it down. Now it became more than a trite platitude; it became a part of his life, his wisdom.

You probably know plenty of platitudes, and you probably agree with every one; but somehow you don't think of them at the right time. By learning the lesson from life itself— your own life—it becomes your wisdom, not

Emerson's or Benjamin Franklin's or some famous philosopher's.

Another entry in this businessman's Wisdom Book read: *Today I learned that the only way to conquer fear is to do the thing one fears.* This resulted, too, from a life-experience in which he discovered that when he actually plunged into doing a thing that he had been afraid of and putting off and making excuses about, he not only handled it easily, but he had a feeling of personal accomplishment, a kind of inner satisfaction that is hard to describe.

He told me that another entry read: *Today I learned that the subconscious mind is like a bank. Every affirmation or statement of Truth deposited in it stays there and gathers interest.* He said this thought came to him as he was standing at the teller's window waiting to make a deposit. He knew that the subconscious mind records and keeps every thought we think, and relating Truth to this very real and personal experience of depositing money that would be safely kept and gather interest, well, it made the power of the subconscious mind much more real and personal to him.

I have just been giving you examples of what we might call general gems of wisdom that come to you as you review your life experiences of the day. But you will find many insights coming to you of a much more personal nature—little ways of handling your work easier, of handling difficult people, or boosting your sales, or getting your student's cooperation if you are a teacher.

Here is one that is helpful, and if you will write it down, you can make it yours. Something my friend had said had been grossly misinterpreted by the one to whom he said it. That person had passed on the mistaken interpretation and a lot of misunderstanding resulted. That day in his Wisdom Book he wrote: *Today I learned conversations are often re-said. So always speak as if 100 people were listening.*

Remember, wisdom is gained from within, and we extract it from our own life experiences through the principles of solititude and introspection, and by applying the stop, look, and listen technique. *Stop* all feverish running to and fro, both physically and mentally; slow down to a walk, then stop completely. Find yourself a quiet and private place and promise yourself, force yourself if necessary, to push the problem out of your mind and to think about the power and presence of God instead.

Look at what? Your problem? No! Look through your problem, past your problem, and become aware of the presence and constant activity of God. To look or to see means more than looking or seeing with your physical sense of sight. When someone explains something to you, you say, "I see!" You do not mean you see something with your eyes, you mean you see it with your mind; you understand.

This is the way in which I mean to see or look past the appearance of your problem to the activity of God. Become aware, or understand that God is present and invisibly working toward a right and perfect solution to the unpleasant facts of your problem. It is difficult to describe feelings. You have to try to put them into pictures. To me, the feeling of looking past the seemingly solid and unchangeable facts of a problem to the activity of God is like battling ten men: Although they may not have you licked yet, you are pretty near the end of your strength, and then you look up and see a great host of your friends coming to help. You are still in the midst of the battle, but the whole picture has changed. You fight with a new enthusiasm. You have the winner's attitude that it won't be long before the enemy is defeated.

This is what seeing beyond the facts to the ever-present, miracle-working, mountain-moving power of God will do to you. The facts of your problem are still there; but you aren't. That is, it isn't the same you anymore. It isn't the cringing fear-obsessed, panicky you anymore. It is a new, strong, grateful, undaunted, confident you.

Listen to what? Listen to God! We are prone to confuse listening with hearing, but there is a difference. Hearing is a physical experience only. Listening is a mental experience. We hear with our senses—our sense of hearing—but we listen with our minds. For instance: You may hear a radio program and not listen. You could be busy driving your car or simply sitting in the next room from where the radio is playing. You hear the sound, but it falls on "deaf ears" as we say, meaning there is no related mental activity. We aren't listening.

Listening is a creative experience in which outer sounds are converted into personal meanings. When we listen to the sound of a cricket, a whole flood of memories and feelings streams into our minds. When we listen to what someone is saying, we hear much more than the words. Things we have read come to mind; pictures and events in our lives enter our thoughts; and new ideas or view-points, new inspiration or resolve spring up from within. Listening is more than hearing; it is a thrilling, creative, uniquely personal experience. Two people listening to the same words will get two uniquely different and personal messages.

Just exactly what your listening will tell you, I do not know. But I do know that when you employ this spiritual technique to touch the source of wisdom within you, something good will come of it, especially if you have learned to record your thoughts in your personal Wisdom Book. *Today I learned that wisdom is revealed to me when I stop (find a quiet place to relax), look (become aware that I have my being in a tremendous energy field), and listen (see facts in a new light), as wisdom and guidance come through to me.*

Relaxation

Ponce De Leon spent fruitless years looking for a fountain of youth. Today we are begining to discover that the youth-sustaining elixir is not in some faraway geographical location but very close at hand, even within us. Relaxation is the key to physical, mental, emotional, and spiritual health. Health means more than just the prolongation of life. Health means wholeness in every department of our being. Health means not only being alive but being vitally, productively, happily alive.

Medical science gives labels or names for the diverse diseases and illnesses that beset mankind. Many of the labels are Latin and practically unpronounceable to a layman, but they are impressive. Some people are funny. Many of them like to have labels for whatever is wrong with them. If they pay good money for a doctor's call, they feel they are at least entitled to a label or a name for their lack of health and well-being. I don't believe in this at all. Doctors have told me that diagnosis is much more difficult than treatment; yet people expect the doctor to identify immediately a variety of vague symptoms under the correct label.

Why do we need labels anyway? It is only important to the one who is treating us. But we accept the label and pin it on. "What did the doctor say?" friends ask. "Oh, I've got such and such!" we reply. And usually the next step is to look up our label in a book where we excitedly find, as a rule, that with a little imagination we could qualify under some of the many symptoms listed—and then we accept the label with even more conviction.

As far as I'm concerned there is only one label to the opposite of perfect health, and that is "a physical challenge!" When you find yourself facing a physical challenge of any kind, the first thing to do is to go to the master Physician within in prayer. Make contact with the source of all life within you. Make contact with the source of all wisdom. You might pray something like this: *God's pure and perfect life is flowing through me now to heal and restore. God's unerring wisdom is guiding me into the right and helpful outer steps to take. I am grateful!* Then relax. As your life unfolds moment by moment, you are carried toward outer action of some sort. Take that action with faith and confidence, knowing that a power and wisdom greater than your own is taking personal charge of your "case."

The next step to take after prayer is relaxation. Let go of your fear. Let go of your sense of helplessness, and let God take over. Physical healing is something that God knows a lot more about than we do; relax and trust the divine Physician. Once in a consultation a Truth teacher said to the person who came for help, "I can see your trouble. You've got the Three T's." "I have, what's that? Is it serious?" he asked. "It can be serious, but it can be arrested with proper treatment," the counselor answered. "When someone has the Three T's it means they are tense, tired, and terrified."

If you have the Three T's, here are some ways of clearing up the condition. Remember that there are four major areas to your being: physical, mental, emotional, and spiritual. To overcome tension, tiredness, and terror you need to relax in all of these areas. Let's take them one at a time.

Physical Relaxation—Slow down, take it easy. I have often said that I seem to accomplish more when I have some bug to fight off with Truth, some physical challenge, because I slow down. I go at half speed, and when it is time to lock the office and go home I am always surprised at the amount of work I have accomplished and the ease with which it was done. Just like a well-tuned car or boat, we have a cruising speed at which we experience peak performance. High speeds wear out the engine, and continuous low speeds waste fuel and get us nowhere. Start slowly and find your "cruising speed."

Exercise is a great relaxer. I am a believer in some of the simple Yoga exercises. The shoulder stand helps the circulation, and then there is the corpse pose in which you just lie flat on the floor on your back with your arms outstretched. Deep breathing is a great relaxer. Take a deep breath through your nose, first filling yourself with air, then letting it out slowly.

One of the places where tension shows most is the back of the neck. Take time to slowly roll your head in a circle, first one way and then the other. Treat your eyes to a rest period, too, by rolling them around clockwise and then counterclockwise; then cover your eyes by cupping your palms gently against them for a few moments while you bless them or make an affirmation of Truth. Then massage them gently.

If you are asking what has all this to do

with religion, I don't blame you. Years ago I would have said the same thing. But I have become convinced that this body of mine, and yours, is a temple of the living God. Look how well we take care of an outer temple or church building. People give money to their church for a new roof or a new paint job, and they feel they are giving to God, and they are. Workers who help clean a church feel that they are rendering a service to God, and they are. Then isn't respecting and blessing and taking care of our wonderful physical bodies, the original and perhaps only real temple of God (at least according to Paul), a form of respect for God and a service to God?

We are coming to realize that we cannot separate ourselves into departments and say that the physical is the lowest department and the spiritual in us is the highest. We are children of God, wonderfully made creations of God.

Mental Relaxation—The key word for mental relaxation is nonresistance. All day things may irritate us and make us nervous and tense. The boss makes some remark that disturbs us. Or it might be a customer who was particularly sarcastic or demanding. Perhaps the screaming children in the yard wear out our nerves, or someone being very selfish causes us to change some plans we had been anticipating. Myriad things sandpaper us daily.

We can't always control other people, but we can always control ourselves. We can't always control outer conditions, but we can always control our inward responses to outer conditions. In Proverbs we read: *He who is slow to anger is better than the mighty, and he who rules his spirit than he who takes a city.* (Prov. 16:32) This is true, because when you refuse to become disturbed, you exercise a seemingly magic power over other persons and outer conditions. Your calmness quiets the choppy sea of destructive mental vibrations in the same way that Jesus calmed the storm and the minds of His disciples in the boat on the Sea of Galilee. It is the very same principle.

Say to yourself, "Peace be still," and you will find that peace relaxing your physical body and flowing out through your thought waves to restore order and harmony in the outer conditions. Nonresistance is the key to mental relaxation and mental health. Resistance makes heat, and heat causes wear (as any engineer will tell you). Have you ever said, "I'm all worn out and I didn't accomplish a thing"? I have. And I know that such a feeling means that I have been resisting things—the clock, people, circumstances.

It is a rule of electricity that the greater the resistance in the wiring, the less power is available at the point of need. The same law holds true on the mental plane. We diminish our potential as conductors of God's power and wisdom and love when we mentally resist.

Here is a suggestion for helping to make fast and pleasing progress in training yourself to practice nonresistance all through the day, every day. When you first open your eyes in the morning, and perhaps while you are doing that preliminary stretching in bed to tone up the muscles that have been restricted for seven or eight hours, say to yourself: *All day long I refuse to become upset, irritated, or angry. I will remember not to react, but to act!*

Never "react," always act out of a center of calmness, and your action will be wise and intuitively guided. The reason for making this affirmation immediately upon awakening is twofold. First, when you wake up, your mind is in that threshold between sleep and waking. This is the perfect mental environment for programming your subconscious mind. So what you speak to it at that time will make a much deeper impression than saying the same thing in the middle of the day.

Secondly, making this statement as almost your very first conscious act will give you a head start on the many challenging situations that come up each day. Instead of waiting until something upsetting happens (and it often will), you are preparing yourself ahead of time, almost anticipating it, and you will be ready with your calm response if it comes.

Emotional Relaxation—Let's see how we can put things in order in the emotional department. Emotions that create tension are hate, fear, resentment, jealousy, self-pity, anger, and—well, you know all those devastating negative feelings. Yielding to a destructive emotion is just like taking poison. They have repercussions in your physical body that are harmful. At the risk of revealing myself, let me use the following as an example.

Once in a while Elizabeth, my wife, and I have an argument. I suppose I should say a misunderstanding, but I'm sure you know what I mean, especially if you are married.

The next morning I often have a terrific

headache and feel generally tired and ill. Believe me, getting emotionally upset over anything is really destructive. On the other hand, the emotion of love is the greatest healing power there is. So if you are like Elizabeth and me and have occasional "misunderstandings," always be sure you "kiss and make up."

I read a story about a girl who sought counsel because she was having constant headaches which were always accompanied by fever. In her conversations with the counselor he noticed that she used the term "burns me up" continually. Her sister-in-law burned her up; her boss burned her up; her tough luck in life burned her up! And her good old subconscious mind was obediently following her orders—headache and fever were literally burning her up.

Forgiveness is the greatest emotional relaxer. When you forgive, your emotions give a great big sigh of relief and unwind the tentacles that tighten your muscles and nerves and cramp your ability to think clearly. Emotions are good; they are the taste buds of life. They allow us to taste and enjoy the good that God has prepared for us, His children. But when we abuse our emotions by indulging in hatred, anger, fear, or resentment, they literally turn on us and rend us.

The girl who thought she was hurting others by running them down and then saying, "They burn me up!" was in truth and in fact only hurting herself. Many times I have heard people say, "Why does this have to happen to me?" A good place to look for the answer is in the emotional department. This is a kind of hidden or secret department because nobody knows whether or how much we get angry inside, or fearful, or resentful, or jealous. It is so easy to rationalize a storm of anger by saying to ourselves, "Well, who wouldn't get angry over such an injustice, or such ignorant, selfish behavior?" No matter how we excuse or rationalize our negative emotional reactions they are still setting into motion negative causes which must result in negative effects, negative conditions.

One evening I decided to watch the news on television before going to bed. Wow, what an experience that was. The news is consistently filled with reports of accidents, controversial issues in which you find yourself taking sides and getting inwardly upset, and reports of violence that tempt one to become angry and hostile at the perpetrators of the violence. Then we go to bed with all these negative emotional pictures and mental states churning in our subconscious minds.

If you must expose yourself to bad news and temptations to respond with wrong emotions before retiring, make sure you have a good meditation time as you lie in bed before going to sleep.

Emotional relaxation is very important, and we don't always realize that our emotional sides need relaxation. So be on the alert for the parade of temptations to arouse wrong emotions in you such as newspapers, speakers, television commercials, politicians, and special interest groups.

The law of replacement is the key to relaxing emotionally. For instance: Replace a feeling of hate or resentment with love and forgiveness. No, it's not easy; but it is possible. Replace the poison of fear with a feeling of faith that God is a very present help in time of trouble and is taking care of you. Replace a feeling of self-condemnation with a feeling of self-approval. We are children of God, and regardless of our past mistakes or failures, God approves of us, God loves us and has faith in us.

Spiritual Relaxation—This means prayer. Take time frequently to get still and remember the source of your being—God, Life,

Spirit, the universal I AM (or whatever name you choose to call that indescribable something that gives you life, consciousness, the ability to think and choose, the energy to act). Spiritual relaxation, or prayer, connects us with the inner source of wisdom and power. When I start to prepare a Sunday lesson, or a Dial-a-Prayer message, I take that moment to get in tune with the universal I AM in prayer.

Get into the habit of taking that moment before you start any task. You will find it helpful to repeat the Scripture: *"Be still, and know that I am God. . . ."* (Psalms 46:10) And there will come flooding into your awareness the realization that God is the universal I AM that is expressing in you and through you as your individual I AM. When you take time for spiritual relaxation, strange and wonderful things happen. Many times when the job you had to do is completed, you find, in looking back, that you did things you didn't consciously or intellectually plan. Yet it looks as if you must have been able to see into the future from the way you handled the job. You see, in God there is no dimension of time, and when you take time to get connected to the all-knowing mind of God, the future and present are merged into one.

Use these key words to remind yourself to exercise the power of relaxation in every area of your being:

Physical — Exercise, deep breathing
Mental — Nonresistance
Emotional — Forgiveness
Spiritual — Meditation

Persistence

I am convinced that many of our prayers are not answered as we wish because we are too timid to be definite, persistent, and even insistent about our asking. We need only to be sure that the thing we pray for is not wrong in itself, and that our receiving it will harm no one else. Then we can and should be firm about expecting a "yes" answer to our prayers. There is good, substantial evidence to support this truth based on Jesus' own teachings.

In Luke, we find Jesus teaching a parable about a man who beseeches his friend at midnight for three loaves of bread. Even if the man will not arise from his bed and grant the request out of friendship, Jesus says, he will do so because of the asker's "importunity." Importunity is defined in the dictionary as persistence in solicitation. Jesus is clearly teaching here that importunity in prayer, or persistent solicitation, is both valuable and necessary at times.

Many people give up rather than importune God. They alibi that it must not be the Father's will for them to have the health, prosperity, or harmony they seek. If the thing we pray for is not wrong in itself and it will harm no one else, then it is God's will. The very desire that gave rise to your prayer was from God. As H. Emilie Cady says in *Lessons in Truth: Desire in the heart is always God tapping at the door of your consciousness with His infinite supply—a supply that He has prepared for you and you are ready to receive.*

You may have misinterpreted the desire, but that is all right. If you pray persistently for the desire as you presently understand it, God will guide you into a recognition and realization of the true desire. Be assured that God's will is always good. For too long many persons have associated God's will with disaster or hardship. Even our legal documents still use the term "act of God" to determine a certain type of catastrophe! How foolish; how paradoxical! God is good and only good. If we want to look for the cause of any hurtful experience, we must look someplace else.

A certain woman who never gets a happy, decisive answer to her prayers, admits that she phrases them something like this: "Oh God, make me well and take away these bad headaches, unless it is Your will for me to suffer for my past sins and mistakes."

Now, unless we know that God is perfect life and His will for us can only be for increasing health and strength, we shall not get very far with our prayers for healing. We are in error by questioning or doubting what God's will is for us when it comes to health, abundance, harmony, or peace. These things are our natural birthright as His heirs. We have been told: "*. . . it is your Father's good pleasure to give you the kingdom,*" (Luke 12:32) and surely in the kingdom there are no sickness, lack, or sorrow. So, when praying for a good purpose, it is our duty and responsibility to pray the prayer of faith firmly and with conviction. Whatever it is that you need or greatly desire, make a fresh start and with renewed faith affirm: *I claim my good and I press my claim!*

Here is a modern parable to point out why persistence is necessary. Peter came to the door of his good friend, seeking a favor. He had with him his two large dogs. As the man began to knock on the door, the dogs set up a terrific howling. After knocking two or three times and receiving no answer the man went sadly away. "My friend has forsaken me," he lamented. "He opens his door to others but not to me." Sometime later Peter met his friend in the marketplace. When Peter told him how disappointed he had been that his good friend would not answer his knock when he was in trouble and had a great need, the friend replied, "Why, Peter, you know I would give you anything you asked for, but I didn't hear any knock. About the same time you say you knocked, I remember hearing some dogs barking fiercely. Could they have drowned out your knock?"

The dogs represent our fears and doubts, or perhaps our subconscious feelings of guilt or unworthiness to receive. Our prayers may at first not be heard because of the disturbance of our own fears, doubts, or other subconscious mental and emotional blocks. Keep knocking, keep praying, keep importuning, and there will come a time when the dogs (your doubts and fears) quiet down, or at least take a rest; and then your knock will be heard and answered quickly!

The trouble is always in us, not in God. The more we stick to our affirmations of Truth, the more we impress our subconscious minds with Truth; and this, slowly perhaps, but relentlessly, dissolves those negative blocks of doubt, fear, and guilt from our subconscious minds or feeling natures. It quiets the frightened dogs, and our knock, or prayer, is heard and answered.

Look at it this way. The longer it takes to have a prayer answered the more we are cleaning and spiritualizing our subconscious minds *if* we persist in our affirmative prayers. We are piling up wealth in our spiritual banks; wealth that doesn't rust or rot, nor is it affected by inflation! It is ours forever, and when a future challenge comes to us, we will overcome it much easier and more quickly because of our persistence in our present challenge.

Another reason not to give up on prayer once we are sure that the thing is not wrong in itself and that it will hurt no one else, is that God might be "working on it." That is, certain other things might have to be brought about first, or certain foundations laid, or perhaps something in us has to be changed before we are ready to happily and easily handle the desired good.

I will always remember an episode in an old television series, Maverick, that helps me to be patient while God is "working on" the answer to my need or desire. In this episode, Maverick just sat and whittled in a rocking chair on a veranda throughout most of the episode, even though he was in serious trouble.

Actually he had sent messages to friends

who were busy at work behind the scenes arranging a scheme to get him out of his trouble. But not knowing this, all the townspeople wondered how he could be so calm about his trouble and just sit there and rock and whittle. When they would ask him when he was going to do something about it, he would only reply, "I'm working on it!"

Finally his friends completed their arrangements; the trap was sprung, and the real guilty party was apprehended. Maverick calmly laid down his whittling and walked away, his problem solved. In the fade out he said over his shoulder to the astonished busybodies, "I told you I was workin' on it."

Concentrating on and working with Truth doesn't demand all of our time, but it does demand persistence and regularity. For instance, it isn't necessary to meditate for hours. It is only necessary to meditate for a few minutes. If we take a pail full of water and throw it on a rock once a week, we won't make a dent in the rock. But if we could somehow divide those pails of water into drops and then just have one drop hit the rock at a persistent and regular interval for a week, we would eventually wear a hole in the seemingly unyielding rock. The strength of the drop of water is in its unrelenting persistence.

I have taught and proved this same persistence principle in fulfilling the prosperity principle of "as you give so you receive." For instance, if we give five dollars a week regularly and persistently for fifty-two weeks, we develop a prosperity consciousness or release the power in the law of giving and receiving much more powerfully than if we give 260 dollars once a year. So meditate just a few minutes, but do it every day, without fail, regularly, persistently, and watch the energies begin to rise out of the deeper levels of the well of Self. Mark it down each time you do. We keep all kinds of records for the Internal Revenue Service and businesses, why not for our spiritual lives?

It is the same with the power of the word. We don't have to set impossible goals of not speaking a negative word for an entire twenty-four hours. That is reaching too high, and we are likely to end up failing and feeling guilty. But we can put up some sort of sign or card to remind us to at least speak more positive words each day; and if the end of the day nears and we have forgotten about our resolve, we can talk to someone with a definite goal of speaking only positive words. If there is no one to talk with, we can write a letter to someone in which we use only happy, faith-filled, positive words!

Be as persistent as the widow in the parable Jesus tells in Luke 18:2-8: "... *In a certain city there was a judge who neither feared God nor regarded man; and there was a widow in that city who kept coming to him and saying, 'Vindicate me against my adversary.' For a while he refused; but afterward he said to himself, 'Though I neither fear God nor regard man, yet because this widow bothers me, I will vindicate her, or she will wear me out by her continual coming.'* "

Then the Lord said: "... *Hear what the unrighteous judge says. And will not God vindicate his elect, who cry to him day and night? Will he delay long over them? I tell you, he will vindicate them speedily....*" As you can see, the promise that our prayers will be answered is implicit in the last two sentences, "*Will not God vindicate his elect? I tell you, he will vindicate them speedily.*"

The widow's stubborn, persistent attitude wouldn't allow the slightest thought of giving up regardless of the fact that there were no outer signs of progress. This is the attitude, Jesus is saying, that we must have in order for God to fulfill His end of the promise (that of bringing about the perfect answer to our needs or desires).

Here is how one woman applied this to her specific problem. I am sure you will see the principle involved, and how to use that principle in a specific problem in your life that seems to defy spiritual solution. This lady called with the complaint that no matter how she tried she simply could not get a realization of God's Presence the way she once did. In fact, she could not seem to get still within anymore. She was tense and nervous. She explained further that something had happened about a year ago in which she made a decision (against her inner feelings) which committed her to a course of action leaving her with practically no time for spiritual meditation and study. She dwelled on this, what she thought was a terrible mistake, and blamed her present spiritual barrenness on it.

During the course of the conversation, she repeated over and over how she had prayed and prayed, and how she had gotten no results. Well, the first thing was to invoke the spiritual law of release. We talked of the importance of and technique for releasing the past. If only we could realize that we cannot change the actions of the past, but what we can change are the results of the actions of the past. How? In only one way . . . by stepping up, so to speak, our spiritual endeavors in the present! But, she insisted, she had prayed and nothing had happened.

Do you begin to see the widow of Jesus' parable entering the picture? At many points in that widow's campaign of getting the judge to vindicate her, she too, could have stopped and complained, "I have asked and asked. I have done everything I can think of and still there isn't even the slightest sign that my efforts have done any good! What should I do? What should I do? And what would the answer be? The answer is contained in the story of what the widow actually did. She kept asking! She kept working! She never allowed herself to think of the possibility of giving up!

This is what the lady I talked with decided to do. This is what you must do if you say you have prayed and prayed about your challenge, that you have done everything. You must keep praying affirmatively!

Let me put it in the form of a mental movie. Picture a young man who was exploring a cave when a slight landslide covered the entrance. As your mental movie opens he is swinging his pick against the rocks that cover the exit, and perspiration is running down his face. Then he stops. He puts down his pick. He is the picture of dejection, depression, hopelessness, and fear. Now, he looks out from the movie at you and says, "Tell me, help me, what should I do? As you see, I have tried and tried until I am so very tired. What should I do?" What would you tell him? What could you tell him but to keep digging, keep working, keep trying? As long as he does nothing, there is no possible chance of reaching his goal.

This is the answer I give to myself and to others when they have prayed and prayed and nothing has happened as yet: Keep praying; keep affirming the Truth. The Principle is true. There is no question but that God is. God is good and God wants me to have the perfect answer just as much as I want it. It is just a question of keeping on, not giving up, persisting, giving thanks for the perfect answer even though we have to give that thanks through teeth clenched in pain, or make our affirmations from hearts that are heavy with sorrow or palpitating with fear! God will give us the strength to keep working at our spiritual efforts to breakthrough to the answer He has waiting for us. Who knows why it is taking as long as it is? But it is taking this long, and so there must be a right and logical reason. And if we knew that reason, what would be our next step? That's right, to keep on praying, keep on working at it with affirmative thinking.

Let your mental picture of the widow in Jesus' story and the young lad with the pick in our story prime the pump that brings up new spiritual strength from the still center of your being. See in your mental movie the young lad hiking up his pants, rubbing his hands together in determination, and then grabbing the pick and going to work with new strength. Then, stay a moment to watch his breakthrough to freedom! Stay a moment to see the joy and thanksgiving in his face. See the satisfaction in his heart that he had not given up, that his faith had been vindicated.

Nobody knows better than I the burdens and challenges that people, good people, wonderful people, are called upon to face. To be a Truth student or a Truth teacher is far from sticking your head in the sand and saying, "There are no problems; there is only God." Sure, there is only God, but there are heartbreaking problems too! That is like saying there is no such thing as darkness; it is only the absence of light—there is only the sun which is perpetually shining! That's true, but what about those dark places where the sun doesn't get in?

If you are in darkness the thing to do is to get out. From my experience, I have found that force doesn't do it. Running away from it doesn't do it. Crying doesn't do it. Complaining doesn't do it. Intellectual figuring and planning and conniving don't do it. Other people cannot do it for you. The only possible way to solve problems successfully and to live life abundantly is to work with the spiritual principles taught by Jesus and applied in today's language, knowledge, needs, and environment. Persistently work with spiritual principle, and at the right and perfect time your faith will be justified! The power of persistence is truly a miracle-working power. The drip, drip, drip of water on a rock will in time cause the rock to yield. The power of persistence operates in what might seem to be an unusual way. For long periods at a time there may seem to be very little outer change. Then all of a sudden—wow!—there is a huge stride toward the goal.

I remember the time I learned to touch-type. In order to be accepted as a student minister at Unity School, you had to be able to type forty-five words a minute. This was because student ministers also worked in Silent Unity, and in order to speedily and efficiently answer the thousands of prayer request letters that came to Silent Unity daily, each worker had to be a good typist. When I took my first test I averaged minus five words per minute. I told my teacher that this was impossible. She replied, "I know it is, but you did it!"

I practiced persistently, every day. You would think with persistent practice that the rate of speed would increase gradually, a little bit each day. But somehow the law of persistence doesn't work that way. It seems to work in plateaus. For instance, I would stay at a twenty-word a minute plateau for what seemed ever so long. Then one day, unexpectedly and without any greater effort than the previous days, the rate bounded up to thirty or thirty-two words a minute. It went that way until that wonderful day when Vera Tait, my teacher and cheerleader, told me I had made the forty-five words per minute goal.

So keep this in mind if you seem to be on a plateau as far as outer progress toward your goal is concerned. Persistently keep going. You never know when suddenly, easily, and triumphantly you will break through and experience the joy and the inner satisfaction of having your faith in God tested and vindicated.

Thought

Thought is a formative power. We can think ourselves sick or we can think ourselves well. We can think ourselves poor or we can think ourselves wealthy.

When we accept this idea as a starting point, it changes the whole concept of Christianity as interpreted by institutionalized religion. With all the sermons based on and explaining Bible passages, you will seldom hear or read a sermon based on the most important teaching of Jesus, which is: The kingdom of God is within us!

Let me paraphrase Jesus in a way that builds up to this startling revelation. First come Luke and Matthew reporting that Jesus said, in effect: "Take no thought of what you shall eat, or what you shall drink, but seek first the kingdom of God and all will be added." Here Jesus is promising or hinting at a place which will take care of all the needs we so desperately strive for.

Next, in Mark, Jesus says: "The kingdom of God is at hand." We are getting closer. Jesus is saying it is very close to us.

And finally, Luke relates how the critical and curious Pharisees demanded to know exactly when this kingdom would come: *And when he was demanded of the Pharisees, when the kingdom of God should come, he answered them and said, The kingdom of God cometh not with observation ... for, behold, the kingdom of God is within you.* (Luke 17:20, 21 A.V.) This is the spiritual bomb that Jesus dropped on organized religion of that day, and organized religion of today is keeping this spiritual bomb defused!

It is understandable that this teaching has not been stressed. Orthodox Christianity has not wanted it known that we all have the kingdom of God within us.

For centuries Christianity has flourished partially by controlling its adherents. People have been ordered to obey the church and its promise of heaven or hell after death. The church believed that it would have been dangerous for people to know they had the kingdom of God in them. So, this revolutionary teaching was kept under cover, and people accepted the idea that the kingdom of God was a "heavenly" place in the sky.

This concept was so much ingrained that in the early twentieth century, when the New Thought teachings taught that the kingdom of God is accessible now because it indwells us, New Thought teachers were ridiculed and called heretics and infidels.

If the kingdom of God is within us, as Jesus plainly stated, then where can "within us" mean but in our minds? The kingdom of God is the kingdom of mind, not just a little corner of it, but all of mind. It's all there, all the power of the kingdom of God and its righteousness (right-use-ness). Why don't we express it? It is because we don't know how to use it. We are just learning about the mental and spiritual laws governing the kingdom of mind, the kingdom of God.

When we learn these laws, as Jesus did, we won't have another mind. We will have the same mind but we no longer will be ignorant, no longer in darkness. We will have the same mind, but an illumined mind. Then, as Jesus said, we will be able to do the same things He did, for we will have use of the powers of the kingdom of God as He did!

The Promised Land is the kingdom of God (or our minds). The Children of Israel represent our spiritual thoughts. The present occupants of the Promised Land (our minds) are symbolized by the Hittites, the Philistines, the Amorites, and the rest, all of whom represent unspiritual thoughts such as greed, ambition, power over others, and all the materialistic thoughts and beliefs that spawn fear, anger, resentment, envy, and hostility. Metaphysically interpreted, the Bible is saying: Throw out, kill off, destroy these thought-people who are robbing you of your birthright of the kingdom of God, the Promised Land. Take mastery of the kingdom of God within you.

And now, almost 2,000 years after Jesus dropped that spiritual bomb, we are just beginning to realize the import of His words. Stated in modern language Jesus is saying, "All power to form and to destroy, to build and rebuild, is in the mind." Mind is the dominant force of all activity. Science is wittingly or unwittingly joining with the revolutionary teaching of Jesus that the mind is the location of the kingdom of God. Modern scientists are saying that your mind can make you sick. It can also make you well.

The phenomenon of hypnotism gives a teaser glimpse into the potential of the mind. Under hypnotic suggestion a person can feel no pain. He can lift unthinkable weights, or, on the other hand, he might not be able to lift a penny off the floor. Such is the controlling power of the mind.

That which moves mind, or directs the power of mind, is thought. *For as he [man] thinketh in his heart, so is he . . . .* (Prov. 23:7

A.V.) What do you think, deep down, about yourself? That's what you are. That's what the power of mind, the power of the kingdom has brought or formed in your life. Mind is the force. Thought directs the force. Whatever you think, you will become. If you want to be healthy, or happy, or wealthy, look to the inner (your thinking), not the outer.

Biofeedback is scientifically proving the power of thought. Through your mind, your thinking, you can turn off your sympathetic nervous system and turn on your parasympathetic system. You can pump adrenalin into your body, or shut it off, by thinking. Dr. Irving Oyle, an osteopath in the holistic healing area, states that a thought has an electrical impulse. If it is a negative thought such as fear, the electrical impulse in the brain arouses a catatonic hormone which starts the adrenalin. If it is a peaceful thought, the impulse arouses a syntoxic hormone (which is a good hormone).

The barriers of limited thinking are being broken down. We are getting away from the thought that there is an "out there" world and an "in here" world and that things just happen in the out there world, then the in here world has to face it or fix it the best it can. As we discover and conquer the kingdom of mind—the kingdom of God within us—we are becoming aware that the cause and the cure are all in mind. We can change the out there effects by changing the in here cause through the power of thought.

We have for the most part taken our minds for granted. I can remember fragments of my youth. I remember episodes when I felt afraid, when I felt happy, when I felt embarrassed, and when I felt secure. I remember too, that I took my mind, and the fact that I was feeling a certain way, for granted; one had hands and feet, arms and legs, and one had a mind.

I was first introduced to the deeper mysteries and wonder of the mind through my mother. She used to bring home magazines that were called "Practical Psychology" and "Your Personality." The thing I remember most about them is their inevitable personality tests. There would be a series of questions that you could answer with a yes or a no, such as, "If you received a 'Don't open until Christmas' box would you open it right away?" At the conclusion of the questions you would count the yes and the no answers, and a key would tell you whether you were an introvert, an extrovert, passive, active, or whatever the case may be.

My growing awareness of mind advanced to another stage. Through these tests and articles I could see that this invisible thing called mind can, in a sense, be read. We can't read what someone is thinking, but through answers to certain questions, we can get a look at what kind of mind he has.

But with all this growing awareness of the mind through psychology, positive thinking, and hypnotism, nobody thought to ask or seemed interested in where the mind came from and what was the source of its power. It is in asking that question that we come to religion, not the traditional, ritualistic don't-ask-questions-just-have-faith religion, but what is called new thought, or the Truth movement.

New thought is really the old thought of original Christianity that there is only one Mind. What you call your mind, and what I call my mind, is the use of the one Mind. In short, your mind is an individualized expression of the one universal Mind, or God Mind. Jesus said that God's relationship to you is one of Father to child. You are mind; you are aware; you are conscious. Where did this part of you come from? Whatever its source, it would be likened to a parent—a Father-Mother Source. As a physical being you couldn't be here unless you had physical parents. As a mental and spiritual being, you couldn't be here unless you had a mental and spiritual Parent.

The Bible says: *For in Him we live, and move, and have our being. . . . "* (Acts 17:28 A.V.) How can this be, except that we are individualized expressions of universal life and Mind? Jesus said: *I can of my own self do nothing . . . .* (John 5:30 A.V.) He is saying it is the Mind of God moving through Him (Jesus) that does the miracle work. He tried to tell us that we are all points of expression of this one Mind, this one tremendous intelligence and life when He said: *. . . He that believeth on me, the works that I do shall he do also; and greater works than these shall he do . . . .* (John 14:12 A.V.)

It answers the question of why a person under hypnosis can hold three people on his body while he is stretched between two chairs. It answers the question why Dorothea Brande's secret formula in her book "Wake Up and Live" works: *Act as if it were impossible to fail.* In both cases we are getting thoughts and belief that limit the expression of the one Mind out of the way. In one case the hypnotist is invalidating our belief that we can't hold three men. He didn't give us the strength, we did, through the use of the un-limited God Mind or Father within. Dorothea Brande doesn't make her slogan work, you do, through the power of the Father within, the God Mind of you, which previously you had covered over, buried with layers of your own limited belief in your ability to succeed.

Now let's take an example of a self-hypno-tized person, John Doe. John has accepted the belief that he will never really amount to anything. Many conditions and experiences in his life strongly suggest that he accept this belief. He was the slowest in his family in childhood. None of his brothers or sisters who were obviously smarter than he had attained any degree of success, so what was there for him?

One day a still, small voice within him whis-pered, "Don't believe that lie that you will never amount to much because of the seem-ingly unfavorable conditions. The Truth is that you are created in the image and likeness of God. You are one with God and have access to the infinite wisdom of Spirit. You are a remarkable person, and there are no limits to what you can accomplish, except the limits you place on yourself."

Well, John listened to that still, small voice and broke out of his self-induced hypnotic belief in his inadequacy. Then he was free to live the full, successful, satisfying life that a loving Father meant for him to live.

Yes, you and I are what we think. Through thinking we form thought-patterns called beliefs. These thought-patterns or beliefs gather substance or energy and eventually congeal into matter or physical form. Surrounding you now are your thoughts and beliefs "hardened" into form! You are and have what you think. The thoughts that run around in the privacy of your mind seem harmless. But they are not. Your mind is not the totally private territory that you think it is. You can tell the character of your thoughts by the conditions in your life, so lovingly pour the nourishing power of your thoughts on that which you presently have, and watch your good grow and increase.

Nothing in life is free. There is a price for everything. The price isn't in currency, but in consciousness. Positive, spiritually oriented thoughts are the currency of consciousness. Negative thoughts are like counterfeit currency—they may get you by for a while, but you always end up in trouble. But you can be a spiritual millionaire and receive the best life has to offer. All you have to do is weed out those thoughts of doubt and fear. Deny and dissolve those false and limited beliefs in lack and sickness, then fill the treasury of your mind with thoughts of faith in God— thoughts of God's all-sufficiency in all things. Affirm in prayer: *The kingdom of God is at hand; and the coin of the kingdom is thoughts of faith and gratitude!*

Faith

Are you letting outer appearances, other people's opinions, or statistics rule your mind? Your mind is your world. When you rule your mind, you rule your world. For example: Mary Doe has a job that pays just enough to keep her head above water. Unexpected car repairs, dentist bills, and the like prevent her from saving any money for future "rainy days." She feels miserable, and wonders what purpose there is in life. Such thoughts and attitudes often lead to stress and then to illness.

What Mary Doe is doing is letting outer appearances suggest to her (or convince her) that she is weaker than they are and she is helpless to change them. That belief rules her mind, and until and unless it is deposed, her world will continue to reflect or express her belief in lack.

We are constantly letting other people's opinions rule our minds. For example, last winter a weatherman expressed his opinion that a winter storm alert should be broadcast. Supermarkets were swamped with customers and the shelves were emptied. Fear-driven householders bought goods to last for several days. His opinion, as it turned out, was far from correct. He later explained that it had only been an alert, but nevertheless his carefully worded opinion ruled the minds of thousands.

Doctor's opinions also carry heavy authority. Even if the doctor only says, "There is a possibility of . . . " or "We can't be 100% sure, but . . . " all our minds hear is, "I've got it!"

Tables of statistics rule many people's minds! Tables of statistics are great for business, especially insurance, where they are dealing with past trends; but they have nothing to do with the individual. Statistics represent what large groups of people have done *in the past.* What a large group of people you do not even know have done in the past has nothing whatsoever to do with you, unless you accept the belief that it does.

Many people view life as a roulette wheel: Maybe they will be one of the "lucky" ones, or maybe one of the "unlucky" ones. Recently I heard a national newscaster report that one out of every eleven girl babies born this year would develop a certain disease. I could just imagine many parents wondering whether their baby would be the one. Perhaps they even prayed that it wouldn't, but they didn't doubt that one of the eleven was doomed. Remember, statistics tell only the past. They have no power whatsoever over the future, unless you totally accept the belief that they do!

You and I have to learn to think for ourselves. "Who am I?" we ask. "The doctor knows more than I do." Or, in the case of Mary Doe we hear, "These appearances in my life are greater than poor, broke, little me. Just tell me how I possibly can change them!"

Well, maybe the doctor and the weatherman know more than you do. Maybe those appearances do look impossible to change. But that is only because your mind is operating from the premise that you are alone, that you are what you saw in your parents' doctor book when you were a kid, or perhaps in the encyclopedia—a bunch of muscles and organs. You also believed that the brain stores everything you know. The inventory of your brain sets the limit of who and what you can be or do!

If that is our basic mental premise, if that is what is going to hold true for us in our lives, we can draw up statistics of how many times in the past we were unsuccessful, or how many times we were just mediocre successes and say, "See! What did I tell you? Statistics prove that I am just a cut above a loser!" All they really prove is that you are just a cut above a loser when you work from the premise that you are all alone, just a flesh and blood machine, capable of doing only as much as has been programmed into your brain.

Life is scientific. Physical science works like this: A scientist begins with a premise. He doesn't know if the premise is right or not. He *assumes* that it is true. He finds that using this premise causes certain results. Along comes another scientist who says, "Look, you got some interesting and helpful facts from that premise, but what if we use this one? See how many better and more useful facts can result from it!" Out goes the previous premise, or assumption. That's exactly what Einstein did. He threw out the old allegedly scientific premise or assumption.

You can change your basic premise that you are all alone, that there is a God up in the sky someplace that determines your fate according to how moral or immoral you are, or whether or not you belong to a church. If that mental premise is making you feel guilty, unworthy, afraid of a hundred and one things, struggling just to survive, change your assumption, change your premise, change your mind!

Try assuming that God is universal Mind, and that your mind is one connected with universal Mind. The kingdom of God of which Jesus spoke is within you, accessible to you. Try assuming that there is a law of mind action: What you think or form in your mind tends to take form or to express in your life. Notice that all these assumptions that have been suggested are taught by Jesus.

Here is where faith comes in. Faith is the will to test—to try—to act on an assumption. Just saying you have faith in your oneness with God, or that the kingdom of God is within you doesn't mean you believe it. Some Truth students of many years say, "Ah, yes. Believe me, you are one with God, and the kingdom of God is within you!" But it is only a theory or a premise until one acts on it in his own life.

Put your new assumption to work. Whatever your particular problem, get God into the picture so that the problem can be met and solved. Affirm right now and at prayer intervals: *The Spirit of the Lord goes before me, making easy, joyous, and successful my way. I am grateful!* These are more than just words. They open your consciousness to the action of God. They place you in tune with the harmonious vibration of the kingdom of God that interpenetrates all things and persons. Things happen that would not otherwise happen.

However, prayer is not a substitute for effort. You still must do what is at hand to do toward the outworking of any challenging outer appearance. But somehow things seem different when you have had a time of inner quietness. You have the comforting feeling that you are not alone. Let me explain that feeling.

Say you had to move a boulder. You heaved and tugged and knew it was too much for you. You would be downcast and discouraged, and there would be a mighty frown of worry and tension on your face. Then along came a great, big, strapping fellow with a friendly smile who said, "May I help you?" One look at him and you knew that you and he together would be able to move the boulder easily and successfully! What would your inner feeling be? The frown would go. All the heavy worry and discouragement would lift. You would say, "Yes, thank you very much. I'll take this end and you can take the other!" In short, you would be happy and eager to get to work.

Faith is like a light, a light that shines in the tangled underbrush of a primeval forest, giving a flicker, a hint of hope that there is a way out, that there is escape. Faith works in your mind and in mine to shed a glow through the tangled meshes of the many distorted, limited, and false beliefs that originated from the outer world and are plastered over our basic sense of identity, the root of our existence, our sense of "I" or "I am."

No matter what happens to or around you, you must cling to your candle of faith that these things are but shadows and underbush that can be successfully overcome. No matter what happens in you—fears, passions, tensions, aching emotions of depression, loneliness, boredom—you must never drop that candle of faith that there is a power, a process, a seed of perfection ever working deep within you, inclining you toward the fulfillment of itself and the fulfillment of yourself.

It is a mistake to abandon your faith because of unhappy things that happen in other lands. It is defeating yourself to abandon your faith in a spiritual universe that coexists with the physical universe because you cannot understand the "why" of a tragedy reported in your daily paper. And the hardest of all is to stick to your faith when appearances in your own life and personal world tempt you to give up the search, to give up the journey toward light and meaning, and to give in to the many escapes and distractions that are readily available.

I am not going to imply that once you have lined yourself up with God the problem disappears immediately. Nothing may change in the outer right away; but there surely will be a change in you! You will see the same problem in a different light. You will see it as an opportunity to meet the hard facts of life from a spiritual level instead of the human level of worry, sweat, and force.

The going may get tough. Many times you may make high promises to yourself. You may have a very real and valid experience of God's presence and willingness to help, but the next morning or a few days later, it all seems gone. Here is where the testing and proving begin. You must push aside those dark and gloomy feelings that arise out of your subconscious level of mind. You must fight them back with patience, diligence, and perseverence. Anyone can give up; there is no trick to that.

On a trip to Unity Village in Missouri, I had occasion to rent a car. The firm I rented it from had a basketful of celluloid buttons on the counter, and printed on them were the words: "We try harder!" Are you saying to yourself, "I've tried to use Truth. I've used affirmations. I've prayed. I've done everything I know"? Then remember the secret of all those persons who have won total victories when things seemed dark and hopeless: We try harder!

You see, working with God is a little different from the way we are used to working. We like to see what is going on. We like to know exactly what progress is being made. If we are having a house built for us, we go out to see it. We examine the structure as it goes up; and if we are doubtful about something, we call the builder and seek a satisfactory answer for our questions and doubts.

But when we work with God, the construction of the perfect answer or perfect outcome is being worked out in the invisible! Humanly we have our doubts about whether everything really is going okay. Sometimes we wonder if anything is going on at all. We yearn to see the progress; we want answers from God. If we want to enlist the help of the spiritual forces of the universe, we must learn to trust, to have faith, to keep our fingers of doubt and impatience out of it!

When we look at challenging, dangerous, or

threatening circumstances in our lives with just our human vision, there does indeed seem to be cause for alarm. And if that were all there is, there would be cause to shake in our boots. But what we see with our physical senses is not all there is. There is a spiritual universe that lies back of and interpenetrates this physical universe of atoms and molecules, and it is plainly visible to spiritual vision—the eyes of faith. We must see right through the atomic veil of "hard facts" to the reality behind the veil, the presence and power of God.

Seeing double, or seeing the facts and at the same time seeing the invisible presence of a power that is mightier than the facts, is very difficult for those who have been thoroughly programmed to believe only what their five senses report to them. It is the familiar battle between the sensual self and the spiritual Self. Sensual means "dominated and governed by the five senses exclusively." Spiritual means aware of the reports of the five senses, but governed and guided and dependent upon the indwelling Spirit of God.

Visualize two universes—the spiritual and the physical. Picture a transparent curtain upon which were painted the physical facts of life, but behind the transparent curtain is an activity that is capable of changing the facts. We can keep our attention on the facts only, or at intervals we can take our attention away from the facts and place it on that activity behind the facts. Only as we continue to look past the facts to the activity of Spirit will that activity work to change the facts. No matter how the seemingly distressful facts want to take all our attention and get us down, we must make a mighty effort to keep our attention on the activity *behind* the facts as much as possible.

Try out your spiritual vision. Look at the facts of your challenge with open eyes—the pile of bills, the chart at the foot of the hospital bed, the letter from a parent or from one of your children that tells of a problem he is facing—and it will seem helpless. Now, close your eyes and feel or realize this Truth: *There is more than this physical universe of form. There is also a spiritual dimension of harmony, power, and wisdom that interpenetrates and transcends this physical universe. With the vision of faith, I see inharmonious facts and appearances swallowed up, disintegrated by the irresistible power of Spirit!*

Success or failure in life can be reduced to two simple attitudes of mind: I can, or I can't! When you look at outer conditions and say, "I can't!" that's the end of that. You can't! And you never will while you have that attitude. But when you look at the facts and say, "I can!" or even, "I can try!" then you have taken the first essential step toward victory, toward unqualified faith in God.

For a spiritual exercise try this: Take a deep breath; breathe it out with the feeling that you are breathing out or getting rid of all tension, all sense of heaviness, all doubts and fears. Now, realize that your sense of identity—your I Am—is one with the universal Spirit of God, the all-wise, all-powerful, all-sufficient Spirit of God, in whom you live and move and have your being. Then repeat slowly enough to be able to think through the words to the ideas behind them: *I totally accept the belief that I am a spiritual being guided by God's light and wisdom. The way to my good is revealed step by step. I am grateful.*

Now you have pushed the button. You have made the contact. The same miracle-working Power that moved through Jesus becomes accessible to you. You have mentally made your attunement to the spiritual vibration of good that underlies all things. You go forth to meet and greet your good. You are working with Principle, and Principle cannot fail. No matter how dark the way might seem to human sight, the invisible forces of Spirit are working to establish the perfect answer which is more wonderful than you can presently imagine.

Intuition

A word that everyone is familiar with but very few understand is *intuition*. The dictionary tells us that the word is derived from the Latin verb, *tueri*, meaning "to look at." Preceded by the prefix "in" we find that the word *intuition* simply means, "to look at in," or to look at inwardly. It is "the faculty of knowing without the use of rational processess." Intuition is information that emerges from within, bypassing or ignoring the reasoning intellect.

The power of intuition is difficult to explain or define because it doesn't make sense to the rational mind. It cannot be tested nor proved by scientific methods, and yet outstanding scientists unashamedly admit that many of their revolutionary discoveries, or certain previously unthought of courses of action that led to solving a problem, came through a hunch, an unexplainable feeling, a dream, or a sort of reverie.

In short, the power of intuition is unscientific; and yet scientists themselves admit that it is a factor in many of their breakthroughs. That's quite a paradox, but we are beginning to understand it. Research has demonstrated that the two hemispheres of the brain have different and distinct functions. The left hemisphere is the reasoning part. It thinks in logical categories. It is the hemisphere we use when we work out a problem in math, for example.

The right hemisphere is nonanalytical. It is the area of dreams that usually makes little sense, at least to the reasoning hemisphere. In a dream, one can be in a restaurant with certain people, then suddenly in a car with other people. We don't question this while dreaming. But if we remember it upon awakening, we say, "What a peculiar dream I had!"

The right side of the brain is the hemisphere of creative imagination. It takes all kinds of unrelated material and "bing!" all of a sudden they are arranged into a new, unique relationship or form. It is from this hemisphere that intuition arises. It is from the activity of this hemisphere that the scientist who has painstakingly searched for the facts and proved every step suddenly finds the full-blown answer in a dream, or while lighting his pipe, or while sitting under an apple tree (Isaac Newton's experience).

For too long most of us have been lame-brained or half-witted. For too long we have given precedence, authority, and validity only to half of the brain—the left half. Anything that didn't make sense to the reasoning left half was nonsense. The nonanalytical right half of the brain, however, is just as useful, necessary, and practical as the left half. Otherwise, why did the infinitely wise Designer of our bodies put it there? It is just that it speaks another language—a language that we cannot understand or do not try to understand because we are lamebrained. We think that only the rules and language of the left hemisphere count in the business of living.

It is through the activity of the right hemisphere that we receive information from the subconscious level of the mind and, in my opinion, from the Superconscious level of mind, or the kingdom of God within. Leading researchers in this field decided, for purposes of clarity, to call the reasoning left hemisphere "masculine" and the nonanalytical right hemisphere "feminine." It is interesting to note that the Bible always refers to wisdom as "she." In Proverbs we read: *Say to wisdom "You are my sister...."* (Prov. 7:4) *Does not wisdom call, does not understanding raise her voice?* (Prov. 8:1) This gives validity to the assumption that the Superconscious level of mind, or the kingdom of wisdom, is reached through the "feminine" right hemisphere of the brain.

How do we learn to listen to the thinking of the right hemisphere of the brain and not throw it out as nonsense? How can we learn her language, make friends with her? How can we have the left hemisphere (the reasoning hemisphere) say, "She is my sister"? How can we develop this power of intuition?

A Unity book, *The Revealing Word*, defines intuition this way: *The wisdom of the heart. It is much surer in guidance than the head. When one trusts Spirit and looks to it for understanding, a certain confidence in the invisible good develops. This faith awakens the so-called sixth sense, intuition, or divine knowing. Through the power of intuition, man has direct access to all knowledge and the wisdom of God.*

This says to me that we develop the power of intuition through meditation. Meditation is acknowledging Spirit, or the Superconscious level of mind, and looking inward (not outward) for guidance and understanding. With patience and persistence, as Mr. Fillmore puts it: . . . *a certain confidence in the invisible good develops.* An understanding of the language of the right hemisphere of the brain develops. Its messages make more sense as we develop more of an understanding of its mode of operation. And this quickens our faith in our heretofore neglected power of intuition.

"How do you meditate?" you might ask. Meditation is the simplest thing in the world, and yet so many people say, "I don't know how. I don't know if I'm doing it right. What are you supposed to feel, or see, or do?" This is understandable because they are trying to perform a right hemisphere activity in left hemisphere terms.

Meditation is simply turning our attention inward—watching—waiting. "Watching and waiting for what?" the reasoning left half of the brain asks. We could answer, "You'll know when you watch and wait"; but let's try to give an answer that the reasoning left half can work with. Let's say, "Watch your thoughts."

If one is new to meditation or out of practice, when he first starts to watch his thoughts, it is like watching a monkey in a cage. He swings, then jumps up and down, restless, nervous. Think of the monkey as your thoughts and your mind as the observer. Just stand at the rail outside the cage and quietly, calmly, and patiently observe. Those flashing, unrelated, sometimes vulgar, sometimes painful thoughts will decrease, becoming calmer.

Be patient. Soon you will feel a sense of peace, of inward comfort. Let your mental fingers pick up a Truth idea clothed in words. For instance: *The Christ Spirit in me is my assurance of divine wisdom and spiritual enlightenment.* Repeat it slowly, silently, reverently, until the words seem to "wear off" and you and the idea are one.

Meditation isn't exclusively a religious exercise. A business person who is deep in thought is meditating. His thoughts aren't running around like our monkey. They are one-pointed, gazing deeply into a particular idea. The solution he is seeking may not always come at that time, but the channel is opened. And while combing his hair or shaving or driving, Wham! Eureka! There's the answer rising up through the channel of intuition.

Intuition is our sixth sense. The five senses of sight, smell, taste, touch, and hearing bring information from the outer world, the physical world. Intuition adds the inner dimension.

Intuition often uses the forms of the outer world as symbols in imparting understanding from within. Dreams, for example, can be valuable sources of information from the Christ Spirit within. Not all dreams, of course; some may be merely distorted adaptations of a television play we saw the night before, or a collage of bits of events and experiences from the shelves of memory. However, recurring dreams and dreams that seem to run in a sequence for several nights usually will be found to have helpful information and a ray of guidance.

There are various theories for interpreting dreams. One that I find helpful is that, most of the time, the people in a dream are symbolic of characteristics in the individual. For instance, if you dream of your Aunt Kitty embarrassing you in front of people, or being an obstacle to you in some way in your dream, your first impulse is to say, "I dreamed about Aunt Kitty last night. I wonder why? I haven't thought of her in years."

But wait. Your sense of intuition may be telling you that the chief characteristic that you sensed in Aunt Kitty years ago is the characteristic in you that is causing you embarrassment or being an obstacle to your forward progress or growth.

Another dream interpretation theory that has much merit was suggested by Dr. Ira

Progoff in an Intensive Journal Workshop I attended. He insisted that we should not analyse our dreams intellectually. We should think about them, write them down. And if understanding doesn't come all at once in a sort of an "Ah ha!" experience, then we should let it go. If we write out the dream, perhaps at a future reading that spontaneous understanding may occur.

Another way that our sixth sense of intuition may use forms from the outer world to impart wisdom and understanding is in imagery meditation. When I am confused by the various options in making a decision, or when I feel up against a stone wall and don't know what to do, I retire to a "Greek temple" or to a "Figure at the Spring."

In the Greek Temple imagery meditation, I visualize a Greek temple in the distance. I slowly walk toward it. I try to see and feel the stone steps as I approach the huge doors. When I enter the temple I realize that it is an oracle temple where the voice of wisdom answers any question I ask. The answers, surprisingly enough, are usually simple, commonsense answers that my sophisticated intellect had overlooked. I have never come away from a temple meditation without some sort of answer or sense of direction that gave me confidence and peace.

In the "Figure at the Spring" meditation I visualize stone steps leading down to a spring. As I slowly descend the steps, I realize there is a figure seated near the spring. The figure is usually someone who represents wisdom to me—a monk, an old man, a beautiful goddess. Then I briefly tell him or her my feelings. Then I wait calmly and patiently for the answer.

It is my belief, from experience, that there is within me and every individual a personal, loving Intelligence that is guiding us in the path of our highest good when we let it. The following is an effective affirmation for getting in tune with that internal guidance: *God's presence within me is my guide. I am positive and patient, as God's light leads me to my highest good.*

When we work with this statement persistently in meditative prayer, we will find ourselves intuitively guided into right action at the right time. Looking back at our lives, we will see with amazement and gratitude that each experience, no matter how trivial or important it seemed at the time, had its perfectly timed place in our unfolding good.

Intuition does not necessarily involve an inner voice giving clear and precise direction.

Once we have paved the way for this spiritual communication system it can and many times does bypass the reasoning left hemisphere, and we find ourselves taking a course of action for no apparent good reason at all. We just "feel like" doing it.

Justice Oliver Wendell Holmes, Jr., who sat for thirty years on the United States Supreme Court, is renowned for his wisdom. In one of his decisions he stated: *General propositions do not decide concrete cases. The decision will depend on a judgment or intuition more subtle than any articulate major premise.* (Lochner v. New York. 1905)

That advice holds true not only for important Supreme Court decisions but for decisions that affect our lives. The wisdom within Justice Holmes' words is saying, "There is no rule book for successful living. But there is the unimpeded clearness of the intuitive process that guides and directs us. Trust it."

Love

If you feel confused and helpless in the hectic world of today, you belong to a large and growing club. The dues are high. They are payable in frayed nerves, tension headaches, and roller coaster rides from heights of excitement to depths of depression and loneliness.

We seem to live in a maddening era of "too much and too many." There is too much to take up our time, our attention, and our interest. There are too many causes we should get involved in, too many injustices we should get incensed about. For entertainment there are too many movies to choose from, too many books to read, and too many teams to keep track of when we turn to the sports page. There are too many styles of clothes, too many kinds of cars, too many stocks, too many analysts, and too many kinds of insurance. In our mad rush to overcome the poverty and deprivation of just a few generations ago, we have overreached and are being choked by the fruits of our headlong plunge toward the Horatio Alger materialism of "rags to riches."

Back in the days when I became interested

in the things of the mind and of the Spirit, it was a lot less complicated than today. There were just a few books on the subject: Trine's "In Tune With the Infinite"; Dorothea Brande's "Wake Up and Live"; Bucke's "Cosmic Consciousness"; H. Emilie Cady's *Lessons in Truth;* and of course, the writings of Ralph Waldo Emerson. But today there are so many books that you could spend the entire rest of this incarnation just reading about God's power within you, about the power of thought and its link with universal Mind.

What is needed is some simplification, some practicing instead of reading, some "being" instead of ceaseless, always-behind-schedule "doing," some inner guidance instead of listening to the chorus of outer manipulators coaxing, tempting, and promising. Yes, it is time we opened our eyes and looked at the world we live in as it really is: promises, promises, promises. Promises of excitement, of happiness, of security, of love—but the insurance policies don't really give a sense of security. The promise of love too many times turns out to be disappointment or divorce; the promise of an exciting special on television turns out to be a montage of distasteful commercials; the promise of success turns into an exhausting and never-ending race with the Joneses.

It is time to come to a screeching halt and change directions. It is time to turn away from books and start reading our own innermost thoughts; they have much to tell us. It is time to resist being hypnotized by the glamor and glitter of Madison Avenue, the soapbox crusaders, and the headline writers. It is time to turn within and discover what it's all about. In short, if we cannot find the answers in the physical world of form, it's time to try the spiritual world of which a Man from Galilee spoke. He said: ... *the kingdom of God is within you.* (Luke 17:21 A.V.)

The first step in the new direction is to decide or determine to have faith in the spiritual dimension of life, even if you cannot see or touch or hear it. Just a mustard seed's worth will do. For, when you plant it or use it, it will grow, it will expand, and it will increase.

The second step is to seek the inner guidance of something the Bible calls wisdom. Wisdom is a bit difficult to describe or explain. One has to use words such as "intuition" or "a still, small voice." It is a spontaneous knowing. It might be called the logic of the heart as opposed to the logic of the mind or intellect. Recently on a television program an oriental priest made a statement that might give a clue to the nature of wisdom. He said, "When you cease to struggle to understand—then you will know, without understanding."

Receptivity to wisdom is cultivated in meditative prayers. It cannot be forced. One must wait and desire it deeply. It is not always consciously recognized. Many times you may see that you were guided by a higher Power only upon looking back at certain things that it seemed to you "just happened."

Now the third step is what this chapter is all about. Take a new look at what your concept of love is. Love is one of those things that we think we know all about, but when we stop to explain or analyze it, we find it slips through our fingers like quicksilver.

We must first realize that from a spiritual point of view, we are love! Love is something we are, not something we do. Or let us say, when we come to realize that we are love, then we can't help but do or express what we are! Why do I say we are love? Because God is love, and God is our spiritual Parent; we are His children, and therefore of like nature. If God is love, then we, His children, are love.

Once we realize this, the next logical step is to eliminate the things that conceal our basic love nature. Those things are our compulsive habits of reacting to circumstances with anger or hate, with irritation or tense anxiety; in short, with any feeling that obscures the loving being we spiritually are. In fact, Paul, in his classic passage on love, places emphasis on the negative reactions we should eliminate, implying that if we eliminate these, love comes through automatically. He says, for instance:... *love is not jealous or boastful* (I Cor. 13:4) meaning, if you eliminate a jealous or conceited response to a person or situation, you automatically express love.

Paul continues: *Love ... is not arrogant or rude....* (I Cor. 13.5) Again, work to eliminate a cocky or sarcastic reaction, and the basic love that you are will come through. He continues his list of negative responses to overcome, as he writes: ... *Love does not insist on its own way; it is not irritable or resentful.* (I Cor. 13:5) This was very eye-opening to me. Heretofore, I had thought of being loving in terms of doing nice, thoughtful things for people, such as helping someone across the street, or making a point of thanking the waitress. Meanwhile, there were plenty of times when I would be upset, or resentful, or irritated at some person or circumstance. I would dismiss this kind of negative response with the excuse that I had good reason to get upset. After all, I am only human. Who wouldn't get angry or resentful or whatever?

I can see now that this was wrong thinking; this is selfish thinking. It is kidding yourself so that you can feel right when you are not right. I urge you to try this approach to love. Try placing the emphasis or your attention on keeping from inwardly responding wrongly to situations and people who tempt you to respond wrongly with irritation, anger, jealousy, resentment, hostility, and the rest.

Let's draw a mental picture. Say you are in a long line at the supermarket checkout counter. You have a million things to do at home and the people in front of you seem to require so much time to get checked out. Often, they seem to take so long in writing out a check to pay the bill. Can you feel the emotion of impatience welling up in you? You usually find that your jaw is set and you are unconsciously grinding your teeth. Well, you and I know from experience that such an emotional state spawns all kinds of negative thoughts. You get hyper-critical. Perhaps you are thinking, through your mental fumes, that you should write the management and chew them out for not having more help available at times like these.

Of course, a few minutes later when you get out to the car you have forgotten about the episode; but your emotions have not. You find yourself tense and hurried. You drive home entertaining all kinds of negative thoughts about why you have to do the shopping all the time, and what thanks do you get for it, nobody appreciates you . . . and on and on.

Let's rerun that mental picture. When we get to the part where you are way back in the line and you begin to feel that emotion of impatience creeping up on you, that's your opportunity. Say to yourself, "You're yielding to this outer temptation to get upset and impatient!" Then dissipate that destructive emotional state. Relax . . . relax your shoulders that were so tense; relax your jaw; and even smile. Pretend an inner Voice is whispering: . . . *what is that to thee? follow thou me.* (John 21:22 A.V.) Now you can see it is not so much that you turned on love, you simply got rid of the negative mental and emotional reactions that were concealing the love that you are!

It is simply a matter of emphasis. Instead

of placing the emphasis on trying to be loving, try placing it on aborting (to use a modern space-flight term) the negative mental and emotional reactions to a person, condition, or circumstance. If you clear out the negative response, the love response takes over automatically. Or, to put it another way, you are naturally a loving person. This is your natural, normal, original state. When you, through your freedom of choice, choose to react to any situation or person in an unloving way, you become unloving. But when you catch yourself and abort that unloving response, you revert to your original state of love. It is just simple logic.

Paul's treatise on love is a practical formula for harnessing the miracle-working power of love. Love will change your life; it will bring order out of chaos; it will cause roses to bloom in a life that seemed like a desert. But the trouble is that we get so hung up on the nice sounding words of Paul's love treatise that we don't really "see" or understand their meaning. For instance, Paul says: *Love is patient* . . . . (I Cor. 13:4) "Ah, yes," we sigh. "Love is patient. How beautiful. How exquisitely said!" But did you ever stop to think that if love is patient, then any kind of impatience is not love? We don't like to think about that, do we? If we get impatient with our kids, or with the delayed delivery of the furniture we ordered, or with the slow clerk at the checkout counter, we don't count that. "It's justified!" we insist.

Paul's treatise on love in I Corinthians does not list any justifiable exception. There is no small print at the bottom. It says that love is patient and kind period! If you want to fool yourself, that's okay; you're the boss. But you can't fool the law of love. If you want the benefits, the results of the miracle-working power of love, you have to fulfill the conditions of its operation. But, lest you feel that I am getting rather stern about love, let me enumerate some of the benefits of a consistently loving response, a response untainted by destructive emotions of hate, anger, impatience, and others.

First, you will feel better in a way that you have always longed for. That is, you will feel as if you are master of your life; for your life is, in a very real sense, a matter of the way you respond or react to the flow of experiences through your life. A sense of calmness will replace the tension, the nervousness, and the anxiety you previously lived with. Your patient, calm, unruffled mind will be sensitive to the rays of the light of wisdom shining from within you; the way a quiet pool is sensitive to a gently falling leaf. The way the fragile impact of the leaf sends out concentric circles on the water, so will the inner light send out impulses of understanding and right action.

If you are sick, you will get well and stay well when you love—that is, when you avoid responding in a way that is not loving. Just as love is your normal state, your normal nature, so is health and wholeness your normal nature. When you stop doing and responding in a way that is abnormal, the Power within returns you to normal.

Being loving does not mean being a doormat, being stepped on or taken advantage of. Love has to do with your inner mental and emotional responses. When that is free of any unloving feeling such as impatience, hostility, revenge, and so forth, you then are open to receive correct guidance as to what to do if it seems you are being taken advantage of. It may well be that you should send a letter to the supermarket management suggesting they have more clerks at a certain hour, or that you inform the Better Business Bureau of certain dishonest practices; but your motive is pure; it is corrective. You feel right about it, and it is helpful, ultimately, to everyone concerned.

You can take corrective action toward a certain unjust or harmful person or circumstance in one of two ways: from a churning emotional basis, or from a calm, inner-directed basis. One way will breed more emotion and tend to destroy you, make you sick, and aggravate the situation. However, taking the corrective action from a calm, patient, kind, and inner-directed basis will take the sting out and lead to a harmonious resolution of the situation and save all concerned from physical, emotional, and nervous strain.

Remember that the spiritual logic behind this approach to expressing love or being loving is that basically you are a loving person because you are a child of God, a spiritual being. And, since God, your Father, is love, you, His child, are love. Frankly, what I am proposing is difficult because it calls for a change in some of your deeply rooted habitual ways of reacting to outer events and people. It is much easier to take the other way of loving; that is, to go on being your usual self, and then every time you happen to think of it, do something nice for someone.

This is one of the objections I have to many of the sweet, beautifully worded, and emotionally stimulating poems about love. They lift you up for a time, and you are very loving until, with the passing of time, the emotional high wears off. It may be in ten minutes or ten hours, but it wears off as you probably well know from experience. The love that Paul suggests in his classic description doesn't wear off. As you peel off the layers of wrong habit responses, the real loving person that you are shines forth more and more through your actions, through your presence, and through your words. Love shines through your hands as a healing touch. It shines through your eyes as understanding and faith. It shines through your smile as a wordless message saying, "I love you and I behold the Christ in you!"

As you start on the spiritual path, first comes faith, faith in the unseen presence and power of God. Then comes wisdom, or seeking to be guided from within. Then comes love, or finding a whole new life awaiting you as you work at developing the skill to respond not with a negative emotion, but by keeping your spiritual cool. Then automatically, love flows out from your right response to bless others and to establish harmony and happiness in your personal world.

Dreams

Dreams—what a beautiful, soft sounding word. There is a promise to it. There are hope and courage. How many songs contain the word dream? Think of some: "Beautiful Dreamer"; "Did You Ever See a Dream Walking?"; "Dream When You're Feelin' Blue"; "A Dream Is a Wish Your Heart Makes"; "Dreams Can Come True, It Can Happen to You"; and, of course, "The Impossible Dream."

People who, in their mind's eye, can see things better than they presently are, are called dreamers. Martin Luther King said, "I have a dream," for instance, changing the course of American history. Would that we were such dreamers, for dreams are the birth of our future good.

A Truth student understands when we say that God dreamed this universe and our planet Earth into being. God is Mind, and all that is, is an extension of the one Mind. And it all began beyond time, when God created the idea, or dreamed the dream.

Many people look down on dreamers, calling them unrealistic pollyannas. And yet, every anticipation is a "dream"; every worry is a dream, for this is mentally living in a world of what has not yet happened. Fear is a dream of catastrophe, illness, failure, or painful embarrassment. That which I have feared (dreamed) has come upon me.

We are all dreamers, dreamers of good, or evil, or happiness or unhappiness, of possibility or impossibility. Some entertain dreams of peace such as Martin Luther King, while others dream nightmares of nuclear war.

Perhaps you have heard a radio commercial with a honey-tongued announcer asking, "How would you like to win a dream home?" I am convinced that you have an infinitely greater chance of obtaining a dream home through depending on God and fulfilling His spiritual laws of demonstration than through the laws of chance offered by the advertising agency.

A dream is an embryo desire. A dream is a deep desire that you hardly dare voice. But it is a desire that bubbled up from the depths of your mind, your soul, your psyche. The Bible says this about desires: *Delight thyself also in the Lord; and he shall give thee the desires of thine heart.* (Psalms 37:4) Is this an empty promise? Are these just nice sounding words, or are we to take them as valid? For me, I see no alternative, either I accept them as true, or else I must admit that the Bible is prone to exaggeration (to put it kindly).

To delight myself in the Lord means to base my life and my thinking on the principle that there is a spiritual reality to life, and that that spiritual reality, or God, cares about me personally. If I do this, all the invisible spiritual forces of the universe will work for me and through me to bring about the fulfillment of my desires and dreams, easily, effortlessly, and with perfect timing.

Actually there is no such thing as an impossible desire or dream. Carried within each dream is the seed of its own fulfillment. Emerson recognized this truth when he wrote: *There is nothing capricious in nature; and the implanting of a desire indicated that its gratification is in the constitution of the creature that feels it.* Look well to your dreams, for they are the first step in the creative process.

What is a dream? Well, it can have several meanings. It is those wild flights of fancy that most of us go on each night. But Webster gives other meanings for dreams, or dreaming. As a noun, "dream" can also mean *a fond hope or aspiration,* and as a verb, "to dream" can mean *to imagine as possible, to conceive in mind.*

To conceive in mind... Conception is the first step in the creative process, whether it be the bees and flowers, or the conception of an idea in mind (a dream)! Tomorrow is a dream! It has no reality whatsoever. There is no such thing as a tomorrow that you can see and touch, or weigh and measure. Tomorrow is a dream that each of us is dreaming from the contents of our inner natures, or subconscious levels of mind; and our dreams come true in the ever-present now.

If you want to change, dream a new dream about yourself! Dream a dream of the infinite potentialities within you as a spiritual being, an individualization of the image and likeness of God, an individualization of God's idea of Himself as man! Dream a dream of the Christ presence as the core, the essence of your being, directing your thoughts, directing your way, and inspiring your dream!

Last November I asked someone what he would like for Christmas. After a long moment all he could come up with was, "Golly, I want all sorts of things!" Well, I said, "Name just one of the 'all sorts of things,' or name the one you would want most."

Dreams or desires are like that. If someone should ask you what desire or dream you would really like to have come true for you, your first reaction would probably be, "Golly, I've got a million dreams and desires." Okay, if you have a million of them, name one. And you would probably reply, "Well, give me a few minutes. I'll have to think about that."

What have you dreamed of being or doing? Perhaps you feel there isn't time to think about it deeply now, but the first time you get a chance to be alone, think about it. What is your dream? What have you dreamed of being or doing?

For instance, if your dream or desire is for a new house, formulate a prayer affirmation something like this: *I totally and boldly accept the belief that God is able and is in fact bringing about the deep desire of my heart to have my dream of a house with a wooded lot, fireplace, spacious master bedroom; these or that which is even better than I can presently imagine coming forth in divine order and under divine timing. I am grateful!*

In this simple verbalized prayer statement, you are saying what it is that you dream, and you are also leaving room for God to give you what in a larger view is even better. Now, you know what you desire, and God knows too. You are bringing the formative power of faith into play through a positive and powerful statement of belief.

Dreams can come true. Following are five steps (perhaps we can call them dimensions because they all start with the letter "D").

Discover. Discover your dream. What is it? Perhaps it has been on the shelf of memory so long that it is almost forgotten. Discover your dream—some of you may not "buy" this, but perhaps dreams can be carried over from previous incarnations. Perhaps you felt the dream a long time ago but put it aside as unattainable.

Our daughter Carolyn dreamed she was an artist when she was five years old, and she painted not only children's paint books, but walls (much to her mother's dismay). When she was six years old she had the courage and confidence to enter a contest of painting a Christmas scene on the big window of the neighborhood bank. Each child was given a blocked off space to paint his or her picture. Carolyn took second place to a much older girl. Perhaps her artist's dream was in her soul from another time and another place. She is now a published artist and teacher at the university level.

We aren't all artists and writers, but there is something in each of us that we can do well, something we can contribute to serve others and to fulfill ourselves. Never say, "But it's only a dream!'' *Only* a dream! A dream is the conception, the seed planted by God!

Your dream may be a new house, or travel, or freedom from care, or fulfilling success in what you presently do, or financial security. We think we want everything. We see a beautiful house and say, "Gee, I would like that!" We see a gigantic console color television set featured in a department store display and say, "What I wouldn't give for one of these." We watch an artist at work and think, "If only I had the talent of an artist." We observe an author signing books and think, "If only I could be a writer." There is no "unacceptable" dream when you acknowledge the Christ presence in you and sincerely seek to be open, receptive, and obedient to His or its direction and guidance. If the dream doesn't seem 100 percent spiritual, who are you to judge? When you stick to using Truth, it will lead to something much greater than you at first thought.

Desire. Deepen your desire for the fulfillment of your dream. Some people say you can do anything you "will" to do. I say no to this! You can do anything you deeply *desire* to do! Desire is a tremendous power. It is the power that gives the "will" its seeming power. For instance, I know people who have the willpower to stay on a diet until they reach the weight they desire. But they have no willpower at all when it comes to saying "no" to anything anyone asks them to do, or vice versa. If there were such a thing as willpower, if you had it in one set of circumstances, you should have it in all. But no, where the will is strong, it is a strong, overwhelming desire that keeps it steady.

So, deepen your desire, for it hastens the fulfillment of your dream. Get interested in things that pertain to your dream. Interest sparks enthusiasm. Read extensively on the subject of your dream. Think about your dream often; visit places or people who have to do with your dream. All these things attract substance to your dream, and your desire deepens as the dream gains substance.

Dedication! Discover, desire, dedication. Dedication means, in everyday language, "work"! Whether it be a famous movie star or a Pulitzer prize winner; a million-dollar-a-year basketball player or a Mary Kay who heads a booming cosmetic business—they worked! They dedicated themselves to their dreams. They worked at them tirelessly.

Mrs. Roth and I had a dream when we entered the forty-foot wide and eighty-foot long concrete block building at 907 N. Dela-

ware in Indianapolis, Indiana Unity in 1956.
I want to tell you about this to make the
point that you don't have to be gung-ho
about the dream you discover in yourself and
that you have a deep desire for. Just be patiently, quietly persistent. The building's inside walls were pale green. All the seats were
metal folding chairs. The nursery was in the
kitchen, and the platform was just outside
the kitchen door. My meditations were punc-
tuated alternately by "Give me that," and
"shhhhhh . . . ."

That was fine for then, but I knew down
deep that it wouldn't always be like that.
This Unity message, in my opinion, is the
greatest thing that ever hit the pike. It was
valuable, it changed lives, and opened minds
to new dimensions of practical meaning to
the Bible. The surroundings for teaching this
message, and for people to listen and learn,
were meant to be attractive, comfortable, and
beautiful. This was our dream. So Betty and I
worked. At first she was my unpaid secretary
and assistant. Later we got a secretary, and
Betty was just my unpaid assistant. We
worked happily, tirelessly, and of course, no
dream is carried out without the help of other
people, and a wonderful team developed. Now
the beautiful 500-seat auditorium in India-

napolis, with no indebtedness, is the partial fulfillment of that dream. Prayer, patience, and persistence fulfilled the dream.

Divine Connection is next, or in the field of electricity it would be DC (Direct Current). We could say God, or prayer, or deity, but divine Connection not only keeps the "Ds" going, but it points out the purpose in every-day language. Divine Connection implies getting God into the picture, and keeping connected with or in tune with God through meditation, prayer, and affirmations of His miracle-working power.

Keep at your prayer work, your meditation times. Work with affirmations until you wear the words off and the Truth idea becomes a part of you. Remember that the attainment of your dream is a process. It involves successive steps. It involves time and timing. It is much like a journey to a particular goal. For instance, a drive to California is a long trip from Indiana. But you have a good car; you know the roads are there; and you know there will be motels to stay in and restaurants to eat in. So you start out on the journey and enjoy it from the first mile, knowing that as mile follows mile you eventually will arrive at your destination.

This is where many people fall down and

never experience the fulfillment of their dreams. They are like a person who a few miles out of the city got to thinking how far California was and how many problems were liable to come up, so he turned around and gave up.

Don't be fooled by the feeling, when you finish a ten- or twenty-minute meditation, that nothing has been accomplished, or that you don't feel any different as a result of it. Remember the one drop of water on the rock. It doesn't appear to do a thing, but drop after drop at regular intervals will give results way out of proportion to the power of a single drop.

The final "D" is *Demonstration!* The fulfillment of your dream or, if not the complete fulfillment, an unfolding fulfillment that will be so great and wonderful and awesome that it is all that you hoped for and more.

Think of the five "Ds" in this way. The first four: Discover, Desire, Dedication, and Divine Connection are the foundation. Arrange them in a square, and then "break out" of the square into visibility by stretching the top line of the square up, and place the last (fifth) "D" there for Demonstration.

Let your theme song be, "I'm a dreamer, aren't we all?" What you hope for the future is your dream. Some of us dream dreams of God's power to perform miracles. Others fill their minds with thoughts of anxiety, hate, fear, and suspicion. Some of us "see" the activity of God working for good behind appearances of hardship or disappointment. Others, with mirror-minds, see only the painful and seemingly unyielding facts. Each is dreaming his chosen dream, and each dream will come true. Such is the nature of a dream.

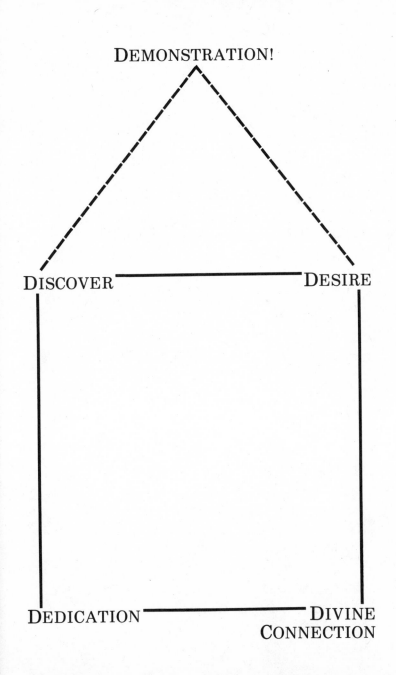

Enthusiasm

Enthusiasm produces energy, and energy is life and power. Energy is vigor and vitality. I don't have to belabor the point. You know that on those days when we have plenty of energy we accomplish three times as much. We never seem to get tired. We feel great physically, and everything seems to fall our way.

On the other hand, when we lack energy, when even getting dressed is a bore and an effort, the entire day is wasted. We accomplish very little, which leads to inner tension and guilt. And that is just the day that everything goes wrong, which, of course, we blame on some power outside of ourselves by quoting the old saw, "Boy, when it rains, it pours!"

What is this thing called energy? Does it come in bottles or pills? Some people think it does. But that is counterfeit energy, a chemical energy that burns up some cells, giving a sensation of excitement. When the fire goes out it leaves behind destruction and damage. So we light another fire and another, until we end up mentally and physically burned out.

True energy doesn't burn us out. It builds

us up. It has been said that the cells of the human body are like little batteries (and that includes the cells of our brains). When pure energy flows through us everything operates at its highest potential. This is why the great statesman and sage Disraeli wrote: *Enthusiasm is that secret and harmonious spirit which hovers over the production of genius.*

Emerson, writing of the energy-arousing capacity of enthusiasm said: *Every great and commanding movement in the annals of the world is the triumph of enthusiasm. Nothing great was ever achieved without it.*

Enthusiasm mobilizes energy. Our minds and bodies contain tremendous amounts of stored-up energy. Scientists say there is enough energy in very small objects to light up a city, or to blow up a mountain. How much more there is in our bodies! In addition to that, we live and move and have our being in an energy field. Again, turning to scientific research, we are told that all is energy. Matter, including air, is but congealed energy.

With all this energy literally at our fingertips, why do we have to turn to pills or martinis or medicine to give us enough energy to drag ourselves out of bed, or to crawl through our tasks of the day? The answer, of course, is that we don't have to. What we have to do is to break ourselves out of the hypnotic suggestion that energy comes from some outer source.

Many people believe that energy comes from sleep. But if energy came from sleep, it would logically follow that if we slept for twenty-four hours, we would be bursting with energy—which we know is not true. After twenty-four hours of sleep, we would grope around like zombies.

Enthusiasm leads to real and lasting excitement. There is something about the very word *excitement*. Recall some of the exciting times in your life, such as the day you were married; or those wonderful, exciting moments at the huge amusement park when you were a child; or the weekend you attended your first college football game.

The word *exciting* seems to perfectly fit every memorable, happy experience of our lives. Let's look up the derivation of the word *exciting* and see if we can find a clue to its magic. We find that it is a combination of the Latin word *citare* meaning "to arouse," and the prefix *ex* meaning "out from." To be excited, then, is "to be aroused out from" a feeling or attitude of boredom or lethargy.

But wait, another use of the word *exciting* is given in the dictionary. It says that it is a commonly used word in the science of electricity or electronics. It means "to energize, to produce a magnetic field, as in energizing a dynamo." My dictionary definition continues, "A dynamo may be excited by a separate machine, or by a portion of the electricity which it itself produces. To render a dynamo self-exciting, various methods of winding are employed."

I think we have a clue here to the secret. After all, we are filled with power—spiritual power. As children of God, or points of expression of the one Power and Presence, God, we have much in common with a dynamo. The dictionary says a dynamo may be excited (energized) by a separate machine; or it may become *self-energizing* by utilizing a portion of the power inherent in it.

Enthusiasm mobilizes energy. We can't make energy; we arouse it. We stir it up; we put it into motion. S. H. Kraines, M.D., in his book, "Managing Your Mind," writes: *Energy cannot be created; but energy which is latent, whether in wind, waterfall, coal, or MAN, can be mobilized and used for constructive or destructive ends.*

Mobilize means to "put into movement or circulation." To put into movement means to motivate. The word *motivate* is derived from the Latin verb *movere,* meaning "to move," and in this word is the key that unlocks the explanation to the cause of our troubles. What motivates you? What kind of energy are you mobilizing or putting into movement to motivate you? Does it depend on outer excitements? I suggest that the reason most people find excitement or exciting experiences so few and far between is that they depend on being excited by a "separate machine," so to speak. That is, they depend on external events or people to excite or energize them—a big football game, a camping trip, or seeing a relative they haven't seen in a long time. This all seems harmless enough, but the problem arises when we fall into the habit of looking for and depending on other people, events, or conditions in order to receive our excitement or energy, or our feeling of being alive. It is a counterfeit energy that comes from this excitement. True energy, lasting excitement (constant self-energizing) come from the spiritual dimension of life, or, as Jesus called it, the kingdom of God.

The false energy that masquerades as the real thing lets us down time after time. Yet we run after it like a dog chasing his tail. A dependency relationship with another person is a good example. When one is with the person, he is happy. When that person is away, he is unhappy, listless, depressed, and feels he is not fully alive. In short, he depends on that other person for motivation, for life.

If he is depending upon this outer source for a sense of feeling alive, he is growing further and further away from depending on the true source of life and energy—the universal life force, or God—and it finds a point of expression through him. When his enthusiasm, his interest, his attachment, his so-called love for that person wears thin and doesn't excite, energize, or motivate him as much, he looks for someone new to excite him. He looks for some other stimulus that will do the trick. This could be drinking or experimenting with dangerous drugs, or, if the monitor of conscience won't permit him to indulge in such outer excitement, he turns to long sessions of playing bridge, or bowling, or golf, or complaining and finding fault.

I am no electronics engineer, but I imagine that sentence from the dictionary that reads, "A dynamo may be excited by a separate machine" implies that if that "separate machine" runs out of power, the dynamo runs down. And so it is with these "separate machines" or outer sources of stimuli that mankind looks to and depends on for excitement, for energy, for a feeling of being alive. Many of us have a habit of running out of power, running out of excitement—then the individual who depended on them is on a "bummer" until he can find some other stimulus to excite him, to make him feel alive.

This is very apparent with drugs. A person may start out on marijuana, but after a while he is tempted to try hard drugs. And when I say tempted, I don't necessarily mean by another person; it is his own craving for the original excitement that marijuana gave that tempts him. The tempter is within ourselves.

The same principle holds true for those outer excitements that are considered more acceptable than drugs. Bridge playing every night excites one—for a time. Then we say, "I just don't get the same kick out of cards that I used to." And we look around for something else to excite us. Or else we continue at the card club, bored to tears every time we go. Bowling, movies, and television may have the same result. They lose their power to excite us, and we once again lose our energy, we become bored, lonely, and feel only half alive.

Complainers seem to fare better. Some people can go on for years and years complaining about everything under the sun and getting excitement from it. But it is a high price. Complaining—which necessarily involves resentment, anger, hostility, and hate—takes a terrific toll on the body. A person can get "hooked" on it. If he stops complaining, he is miserable; and whether he stops or not, he is sick and miserable.

I could go on and on, but I'll let you take it from there. Think about it. How much do you depend on outer things, circumstances, conditions, and people to make you feel alive and happy? If you depend on them, you are enslaved to them, you need them, they rule you and pull your strings. In a sense, you actually become in bondage to these outer sources of excitement. Just as the dynamo that *has to have* a separate machine to energize it, you *have to have* outer excitements. You may kid yourself that they are only relaxations. Okay, if they are, try giving them up for several months, and you may sit around biting your fingernails and "crawling the walls."

The answer, as I see it, is to work toward becoming the second kind of dynamo that the dictionary mentioned, "A dynamo may be excited by a portion of the electricity which it itself produces." This means the dynamo is not dependent on the outer source for energy, and in making the analogy with ourselves, it means we are not dependent on other people or outer events and conditions in order to feel alive and fulfilled.

The way to become excited, or energized, or to feel fully and completely alive is to look to and to depend on your inner contact with that energy field that we call God. This does not mean that we do not play golf, or bowl, or enjoy relaxation in many other ways. We do not retreat from the world. However, the point is, we do not *need* these things. We are not slaves to them; we are free souls!

I realize this is a very subtle point and it takes some thought. It isn't easy to break our attachment, our bondage to the environmental world as the source of our excitement. Our brainwashed egos will give all sorts of excuses and arguments. And even if we see the logic of turning within for the kind of excitement or energy that is lasting and satisfying, it cannot be done in the wink of an eye. You will have to spend some time getting acquainted, being at home in those far reaches of inner space within you. Start tomorrow morning immediately upon arising. Repeat to yourself or aloud if circumstances permit: *I am alive, alert, awake, joyous, and enthusiastic about life!*

You will, of course, get an immediate reaction from your personal ego which is likely hypnotized by your world of effects. It will say within you, "Your body is tired; your mind is foggy; you hate the thought of showering and getting breakfast. Who are you kidding that you are "alive, alert, awake, joyous, and enthusiastic about life"? However, pay no more attention to this seeming logic than you would a hypnotized person who insists the room is freezing because his hypnotist told him it is when you know that the room is actually comfortable.

The Truth is that you basically are a spiritual being. Spirit is energy. The non-physical, spiritual you is alive, alert, awake, joyous, and enthusiastic about life. When you believe an untruth all your life, the Truth seems to be a lie; just as people who grew up in the belief that the sun revolved around the Earth found it impossible to conceive of the Earth revolving around the sun. But try it. Try the Truth. Say: *I am alive, alert, awake, joyous, and enthusiastic about life!* and see if you don't feel the movement, the mobilization of the energy of the life force deep within you.

Then once you are launched on a program of inner space exploration and discovery, once you taste, experience, and make a part of yourself that inner atmosphere of peace and wonder and humility, you will find a new quality to your consciousness. You will find that you are able and look forward to living deeply in the present moment. I don't mean just in your meditation times, but as you traverse the hours and days of your entire life. You will begin to see that eternal life is a question not of length but of depth. Eternal life reaches down deeply into the present moment because the present moment of time is all there is. The past is a memory stored in some cells in your brain, and the future doesn't exist except as an embryo in the now.

The most universal and inescapable law there is, is the law of cause and effect. Where there is a cause, there must be an effect; where there is an effect, there must have been a cause. The present moment is filled with effects, but it is also waiting to be impregnated with causes. We reap in the now; we sow in the now. Or, as Jesus said: "... *the fields are already white for harvest,*" (John 4:35) even though He was looking at a freshly sown field.

Life at our present stage of unfoldment and understanding is, as Paul said, a battle between the powers and principalities of the world, and the spiritual forces and powers within us. The powers of the world do not refer to big companies or big government; it refers to the hypnotic hold the world of appearances has over our minds. We totally accept the material world as all there is. And because we accept it as the only reality, we become dependent upon it. Jesus said, in effect, "Totally accept the spiritual universe, the kingdom of God, the omnipresence of Spirit as the reality. You will then become dependent on it, on God. And, because you are dependent on God, you become what you always have been potentially—a child of God.

We live, move, and have our being in a sea of energy, and we mobilize, or actualize, or activate this energy through enthusiasm. For instance, several years ago I experienced the miracle power of enthusiasm on a tour of the South Seas. Our flight was delayed, and we arrived at the airport in Fiji at 4 a.m. There were no customs people to check us in. The handful of personnel at the all-but-deserted airport said we would have to wait until customs people could be awakened and get there.

There the sixty-five of us stood, our baggage piled high where it had been unloaded. As the minutes grew into more than an hour, we became painfully bored, tired, and tense with repressed impatience. Jane Paulson, a Unity minister, was on the tour, and she started a singing affirmation that went like this:

I'm alive, alert, awake, enthusiastic;
I'm alive, alert, awake, enthusiastic;
I'm alive, alert, awake—awake, alert, alive;
I'm alive, alert, awake, enthusiastic!

At first just a few sang it with her, and it sounded like more of a funeral dirge than anything else. But before long more started to sing and the tempo picked up, until we were all smilingly singing our hearts out with joy and enthusiasm. Because the words are so simple to memorize, the airport personnel joined in, and you should have seen the astonished look on the faces of the customs men when they arrived. They had expected to meet a group of angry, impatient, and tired complainers. Instead they found the place bursting with joy and energy.

You are chock-full of energy. It is waiting to be released. Turn within. Stir it up. Break the bonds of lethargy that have you strapped to a life of procrastination and listlessness. The bonds are mental and are no match for the energy of Spirit. It doesn't take willpower; it takes desire power! Do you really want to be alive, awake, alert, and enthusiastic about life, and work toward the good that awaits you? Sure you do!

Then take that mustard seed of desire and make an affirmation or two directed toward releasing the God-energy within you. Each time you speak the affirmation, a bit more energy is released which will feed the fire of desire. The first thing you know, you will be saying with happy amazement and joy, "What do you know, it works!"

Printed U.S.A.   160-F-9307-25C-3-87